Praise for

SKIRT!® RULES >
>
>
> FOR THE WORKPLACE

"Want a fulfilling career? To be paid what you are worth? To get ahead without leaving your ethics in the garbage? *skirt! Rules for the Workplace* ... is savvy, strategic, and suitable wisdom for any office."

—Jennifer Baumgardner,
author of *Manifesta, Grassroots,* and *Look Both Ways*

"Funny, feminist, and packed with practical suggestions that will make your work life better—and make the workplace in general better for women. I learned something or got useful encouragement on every page."

—Alison Piepmeier,
director of the Women's and Gender Studies
Program at the College of Charleston

SKIRT!® RULES >
>
>
>
>FOR THE WORKPLACE

An Irreverent Guide to Advancing Your Career

KELLY LOVE JOHNSON

SKIRT! IS AN IMPRINT OF THE GLOBE PEQUOT PRESS > GUILFORD, CONNECTICUT

skirt® is an imprint of The Globe Pequot Press.

skirt!® is a registered trademark of Morris Publishing Group, LLC, and is used with express permission.

10 9 8 7 6 5 4 3 2 1

Printed in the United States of America

Text design by Georgiana Goodwin and Jayne Hertko
Author photo by Leigh Webber

Library of Congress Cataloging-in-Publication Data
Johnson, Kelly Love.
  skirt! rules for the workplace : an irreverent guide to advancing your career / Kelly Love Johnson.
    p. cm.
ISBN-13: 978-1-59921-223-4
1. Women executives—Psychology.
2. Executive ability.
3. Leadership in women.
4. Sex role in the work environment.
5. Office politics.
I. Title.
HD6054.3.J64 2008
650.1082—dc22
                    2007006769

*This book is dedicated to all of the bosses
I've ever had in my life,
good and bad, because they made me what I am today ~
*
especially my first boss,
the one who taught me I CAN have it all,
my mother, Ginger Johnson.*

Contents

Foreword

My first real job was in the late 1970s with a staid textbook publishing company, and even though I had a B.A. and a 4.0 GPA, I had to start as a secretary. I wanted to be on an editor track, but I was told that all editors came from the sales staff, no exceptions. At the time, all the editors in my company were men, no exceptions. Lucky for me, I had a great mentor who wasn't scared by my ambition. He gave me challenges and opportunities and took genuine pleasure in my successes. Slowly but surely I was promoted to assistant editor, associate editor, and eventually senior editor and VP of the company. The secretary who took my place was also subsequently promoted to editor, and another female editor was hired from the outside.

That particular glass ceiling cracked and the world didn't come to an end, but I owed much of my good luck to a good mentor. I could have been just as smart but made no headway with a different boss and less enlightened upper-level management, because the "rules" were still made by men. Feminists were kicking down all kinds of bar- GOOD MENTOR riers at the time, but sometimes it seemed as if our power was only suit-deep. At the same time, I have to admit that I was probably a difficult employee in many ways—smart but immature, talented but moody, quick-witted but quick to take offense at criticism. I still wince when I remember some of my pouty passive-aggressiveness. There's no doubt that I could have used *skirt! Rules for the Workplace*— and so could my bosses.

Decades later, when I started my own business in a corner of my living room, I realized that in order to grow, I'd have to hire actual employees. As a loner who loves to sit in front of a computer all day long, I dreaded being a manager. So I made sure I hired people who didn't require a babysitter or a 24/7 cheerleader or a hand holder—women who simply rolled up their sleeves and created their jobs from scratch.

Kelly Love Johnson is one of those women. Not only is she a supremely gifted writer, as you'll discover in these pages, but she is also utterly dependable and frighteningly well organized. My desk is waiting for an archeologist to dig me out; her facts and folders are at her fingertips. I hate confrontation or firing people; she handles people problems with grace, tact, and firmness. Luckily our skills and strengths are nicely complementary, and we have the good fortune to work in an office of other powerful, strong women who aren't afraid of making their voices heard. After reading her book, I think you'll agree with me that Being Kelly is the next best thing to Being Betty, the next new voice to continue the work of Betty Friedan in bringing true equality to the office.

~Nikki Hardin,
Founder of **skirt!** magazine

skirt! Rules for the Workplace is a real-life perspective on feminism in the workplace, with a humorous approach, for young (or not-so-young) women who want to know what they can do to close their own wage gap and break through the glass ceiling.

Because of the women who came before me, particularly my own mother and grandmother, there was never a question in my own life about having to choose between work and family. My single-parent grandmother worked all of her life. My mother, also a single parent, has worked since I was very young—while raising four daughters—and now, in her early sixties, has no concrete plans to retire. I invest in a retirement plan, but also plan to keep writing until I am no longer able to do so (which hopefully will be when I'm in my late nineties living in my villa on the Italian Riviera). Most women today—with and without children, married or unmarried—work because they have to.

Unlike my mother and grandmother, I have not had to face societal reproach for my decision to work full-time and not have children. Before my parents' divorce, when my mother (probably sensing trouble brewing ahead) decided to enter the workforce, she remembers suddenly not being part of the "mommy club" anymore. Some of the friends she had when she was a stay-at-home mom with two teenagers and

Introduction

two preschoolers wondered how she could choose not to spend 24/7 with her children. She felt like she had to leave one club to join another.

There's still somewhat of a dogmatic attitude toward women with children who choose to work full-time. Why aren't we putting our children first? In my grandmother's case, she was. She was the single parent of a three-year-old and had no choice but to work to feed them both. In my mother's case, entering the job market might have had more to do with a lack of fulfillment she felt being a sole caregiver (even before the divorce, my father was often absent), but after the divorce, her working was a necessity, not a choice. I have three sisters who have children, one still married, and not working for indefinite periods of time—even holding out long enough for preschool—was not an option for any of them. They all returned to full-time jobs after maternity leave.

> THESE WOMEN PAVED THE WAY SO THAT THE WOMEN OF OUR GENERATION CAN BE ANYTHING WE WANT TO BE—GLASS CEILINGS AND "MALE-DOMINATED PROFESSIONS" BE DAMNED.

My point here is that we're lucky—not because we have to work, but because the working world is no longer the often hostile place it once was for women. The women's movement, activists like Gloria Steinem and Betty Friedan, and hundreds of thousands of "regular" women just like you and me, fought the good fight for years so that we don't have to suffer insufferable misogynist male bosses, tolerate harassment, or be forced to do "women's work," as it was called in the 1950s. These women paved the way so that the women of our generation can be anything we want to be—glass ceilings and "male-dominated professions" be damned.

So why are we still making less than our male counter-parts? The wage gap seems to be the last bastion of gender discrimination in the workplace, but it's a big one. Yes, we can be doctors, lawyers, engineers, firefighters . . . even (cross your fingers) President of the United States, but chances are good that our wages will fall short of what men in those same professions bring home. Is it because we're unreliable and might end up leaving the workforce to stay home with our children? Most studies (and the ones I've cited in this book) exclude women who leave the workforce to raise their children. Is it because we're not as good at our jobs as men are? Because we're too fragile? Because we have ovaries? Because we might have PMS when a project is due? Because men don't want us to work? The answer to all of the above is an absolute, unequivocal "No."

WAGE GAP

This book was in my head for a long time before I wrote anything down. It appeared here and there in small ways—in an essay I wrote following the death of Betty Friedan in 2006, in occasional rants among friends or coworkers when the subject of the wage gap came up, in what my boss once called "Kelly Charisma's Rules for Work," and in numerous short lists of "Never Do This at Work." I spouted off information randomly depending on the given situation—but my passion about closing the wage gap typically focused on my efforts to climb the corporate ladder and put more money in my own checking account.

In 2006, the director of The Center for Women in Charleston, Jennet Robinson Alterman, asked me to speak to a group of girls on the topic of women and achieving success in the corporate world. The young women were mostly from a mentoring organization that worked with at-risk girls who were raised in foster homes. During the session, I looked around the room at the faces of these girls, who were eager and inquisitive and seemed to be waiting for the one answer that would assure them success as they entered the working world. And I didn't have an answer for them. I only had answers for myself.

In the days that followed the workshop, I discussed my frustration at not being able to do anything constructive to help these young women and others like them with several people, including the center's director and my boss and founder and publisher of *skirt!* magazine, Nikki Hardin. After patiently listening to my various complaints about how colleges don't prepare young women for success, about how society devalues the work of women, about how some employers assume women's work is worth less than the work of men, both women told me the same thing: "You should write a book."

So I did. And here it is.

I'm the QUEEN of MISTAKES

In the months I spent working on *skirt! Rules for the Workplace*, I asked myself the following question hundreds of times: Who am I to be giving advice to young women about climbing the corporate ladder? I'm the Queen of Mistakes, guilty of violating my own rules so many times I shouldn't be allowed to have rules at all. I've dated coworkers, gotten drunk at office parties, cried in my boss's office, not asked for the higher salary because I wasn't sure my work was worth it, and once (just once!), I even baked for the office.

I've also been fired, forced to resign, underappreciated, over appreciated, a slacker, a workaholic, put my job before my family, and had temper tantrums at work. So who am I to tell other people how they can give themselves a hand up and make more money? The book was almost finished before it dawned on me that hey, actually, I might be *exactly* the perfect person to do it!

I've never been afraid of taking risks, therefore I've made mistakes. I was once twenty-three-years-old, therefore I've made mistakes. I've been in the right job at the wrong time, and the wrong job at the right time, therefore I've made mistakes. And I can honestly say that I have learned from all of them. I've thought about those mistakes a lot—particularly while remembering and writing about them—and the conclusion I finally reached is this: **If one more person can learn from my mistakes, she won't make the same ones.** And maybe I won't cringe so much when I remember them. I hope you're that one person.

THE CORPORATE WORLD IS ALL ABOUT SURVIVAL OF THE FITTEST, BUT IT DOESN'T HAVE TO BE A WAR, OR EVEN A DAILY BATTLE.

The corporate world is all about survival of the fittest, but it doesn't have to be a war, or even a daily battle. At best, it can be a series of minor skirmishes, each one either a win or a lesson, not a loss. It's not about us against them or the men against the women (or even the women against corporate America). All men are not to blame for the fact that many women still earn less money than they do. The problem is a lot larger than a "Good Old Boys" club deciding to keep women down. But broken down on an individual level, the problem is not as insurmountable as it seems. My goal with this book is to give you the tools that you need to close the wage gap—not by marching in the streets or forming a union, but by taking the small, manageable steps that will get you from where you are now to where you should be just by closing your own wage gap.

Whether you're entering the workforce for the first time right out of college or sitting behind a desk in an entry-level job wondering why you're not getting promoted, don't let anyone tell you that you can't, that you shouldn't, or that it's too hard. Your career is about **you**; no one else should have the power to discourage you. Keep a firm grasp and a strong foothold on the rungs of the corporate ladder, and don't look down. But once you're up there, don't forget to reach back and offer a hand up to the woman who's next in line. If we all do this, one woman at a time, it might not take thirty years to reach our goal of gender equality in the workplace.

~ Kelly Love Johnson

CHAPTER ONE

BEING BETTY: A FEMINIST SAYS WHAT?

"The problem that has no name—which is simply the fact that American women are kept from growing to their full human capacities—is taking a far greater toll on the physical and mental health in our country than any known disease."

~ *Betty Friedan (*The Feminine Mystique, *1963)*

In February 2006 one of the loudest voices of the modern women's movement fell silent. Betty Friedan died at her Washington home on her eighty-fifth birthday.

A founding member of the National Organization for Women in June 1966, Friedan and Dr. Pauli Murray coauthored its original statement of purpose, which began, "The purpose of NOW is to take action to bring women into full participation in the mainstream of American society now, exercising all the privileges and responsibilities thereof in truly equal partnership with men."

She was a staunch feminist, yes. But I've always considered her more labor activist than consciousness-raiser. From the time *The Feminine Mystique* was published in 1963, until just a few years before she died, Friedan worked to push equal pay, sex-neutral help wanted ads, maternity leave, child care, and many other issues of gender parity in the workplace.

As NOW's president from 1966 to 1970, Friedan led efforts to lobby the U.S. Equal Employment Opportunity Commission (EEOC) to enforce laws against sex discrimination in hiring practices, and to ban employment ads that were segregated by sex. During that time, NOW also convinced President Lyndon Johnson to sign an executive order barring sex discrimination by federal contractors.

In 1998, at an annual Association of Work/Life Professionals conference in Miami, Friedan issued a clarion call to redefine work so that women can care for their children, stating that it is necessary to create genuine equality. She said (and I'm paraphrasing from memory), "Women have always juggled a lot; it's just what they are juggling that has changed."

Considering that what we are juggling has changed, and that the glass ceiling has scarcely budged in response, who will step up to fill Friedan's shoes? Unless you have thirty years (which is how long it will take, according to Economic Policy Institute statistics) to wait for the wage gap to close, I nominate you. All of us, really, should think about being Betty once in a while.

Look how far we've come—in this country, women can vote, drive cars, walk in public unaccompanied, run for office, run companies, and wear whatever the hell they want while they're doing it. But it's not far

What would **BETTY** *do?*

enough, baby, as long as there are women out there who have so few options that they take jobs that require them to perform the same tasks as their male counterparts, plus fetching coffee, stocking the office fridge, wiping the counters, and wearing pantyhose so no one has to be offended by a bare

WOMEN HAVE ALWAYS JUGGLED knee, along with earning less money. As long as these women exist, it is our responsibility to ask, "What would Betty do?"

Being Betty means we are prepared to organize a walk-out, boycott, protest at the drop of a hat, even lose our jobs in order to draw attention to the issue of salary disparity. Being Betty means that we use facts about our actual performance on the job instead of our emotions to negotiate a better salary. Being Betty means that we leave our "need to please" at home. Being Betty means that we insist, as often and as loudly as necessary to be heard, "This is not fair."

Being Betty means that we know the law, that we seek out powerful women and support them instead of running them down. Imagine how much more you could get accomplished at work if you knew, like many men know about their "Good Old Boys" network, that your female colleagues were watching your back instead of waiting to stab you in it. Other women are not a threat. We should be offering each other opportunities and encouragement instead of opposition and envy.

Being Betty means that we don't blame our moodiness on PMS or our mistakes on being "just a girl." We don't talk baby talk in the office. We don't cry until we get home. And we don't bake cookies

> BEING BETTY MEANS THAT WE LEAVE OUR "NEED TO PLEASE" AT HOME.

for our coworkers. A woman doesn't have to act like a man in the office to be considered CEO material. She just has to stop acting like his mother.

Being Betty means that we've done enough research to know that companies actually perform better with a higher percentage of women in upper management and executive positions. Brute strength is required for some jobs, but in the white collar world, intuition, strong social skills, and compassion go a long way. Women naturally excel at managing staff because we balance competence with concern. We consider morale and the bottom line equally important.

Being Betty means choosing your battles intelligently. Fighting for the cause of coed bathrooms may not be as valuable a use of your time as fighting for the cause of promoting women as frequently as men.

Being Betty means understanding that the glass ceiling is not a myth. Although women make up almost half of America's labor force (U.S. Department of Labor), still only seven Fortune 500 companies have women CEOs or presidents, and ninety of those 500 companies don't have any women corporate officers (catalyst.org).

But even Betty couldn't pull off a one-woman revolution. Whether you want to move up the ranks or settle happily where you are, it's difficult to understand how it is possible, in the twenty-first century, for women to be seen as "lesser-than" in the workplace. Sure, some of us work full-time jobs. Some of us have children *and* work—that's two jobs. Some of us have children—and that's one job. However, just the potential that a woman may choose to stay home following maternity leave isn't reason enough to relegate women to a lower position. Should she choose to leave, there are hundreds more standing by, competent, educated, and ready to take her place.

Betty herself was fired in 1952, from Trade Union Service (ironically, a company that edited newspapers for labor unions), when she was pregnant with her second child, because her boss knew she'd want to take maternity leave. She might have wept and decided to stay home and bitterly accept it. But she spent the next several years at home freelancing and bitterly writing *The Feminine Mystique* instead.

The Feminine Mystique was published thirty years before I got my hands on it. One would think, since inroads were made and the foundation had been laid, that I wouldn't have found the book relevant in the early 1990s. But what I did find, as I entered the workforce for the first time, was that the outmoded ideals Friedan argued against were still prevalent. As the product of a feminist mother, childless, and relatively responsibility free, I was lucky to be able to walk away from one misogynist boss who thought boob jokes were the height of hilarity, another office where I was required to wear "one-inch defined heels and nude (not taupe, not black) pantyhose" as part of the dress code, and a third where a male supervisor kept imploring me to "smile, honey." For me, no job was worth compromising my integrity or self-respect. But it wasn't hard to imagine what women who were single mothers, sole breadwinners, or lacking other means of support had to contend with every single day.

Unless you have another thirty years to wait for a fair and balanced workplace, someone has to be Betty. **Find your voice.** You don't have to risk your job to do it. Sometimes people don't realize policies aren't fair until someone else speaks up.

"Smile, honey."

If no one speaks up, we'll continue to live in a world where "acting like a girl" is a derogatory statement. "You're such a girl" means you earn seventy-five cents on every dollar he makes. "You're such a girl" means there's a good chance you won't be taken seriously when you should be. We are girls, we are females, we are women. But don't let them take those things and turn them into reasons why we deserve less, why we should be considered weaker, lacking in intelligence, and run by our emotions.

It's high time to stop fetching coffee because you happen to be the only female at the conference table. It's time to stop wearing pantyhose because some male CEO with a corner office deems it "appropriate and recommended attire." Hell, stop wearing anything that isn't consistent with a dress code that affects everyone in the office, as opposed to just the employees who wear skirts.

Stop being afraid to ask for a raise or promotion—or to ask what you should be doing to get one. If you've done your research and are reasonably certain your pay is lower than

You don't have to lose your job, march on the Capitol, or even carry a sign...

that of male colleagues, don't just bitterly accept it. In the simplest terms, here is what men do that you don't: Have a meeting with the boss. Explain what the desired outcome is. Ask how to get there. It sounds scary, but it's as much part of your financial life as filing your taxes or paying your mortgage.

Other people—other women—made the opportunities we have today possible. We owe them for being able to define our lives by who we think we are, rather than who other people think we should be. But the progress women made in the 1960s and 1970s has not continued. We've lost momentum, and we've lost focus. And now we've lost Betty.

You don't have to lose your job, march on the Capitol, or even carry a sign. You don't even have to raise your voice. Think about your actions in your work life. If you can't name any instances of standing up for women's rights, then it's time to settle up. Be Betty just once this month: Show him where the coffee machine is. Teach him how to use his own e-mail.

Tell him to change your title from "My Assistant" to "My Colleague." Visit Salary.com or Pay-Equity.org and find out if you are making what you're worth. Mentor another woman. Network with other women.

In present-day corporate America, corporate counsel shouldn't have to advise managers who have hiring power not to ask female employees if they intend to get pregnant (or married, or otherwise imply they might not be the best candidate for either of those reasons). In fifty-plus years, we should have made inroads in changing the thinking of corporate America. Do I know women who stay home with their children? Absolutely. I also know men who stay home, women

...mentor another woman.

who have four children and work full-time, women who are raising children as single parents and work more than one job, and childless women who are independently wealthy.

Our ability to bear children should not—and legally, it cannot—have any bearing on our ability to perform the tasks associated with a job in our field. In 1952 it was legal for Betty Friedan's boss to fire her because he'd rather replace her than pay for maternity leave. We have laws now (the Family and Medical Leave Act of 1993, for example) protecting family leave for both men and women, but many of those laws do not apply to private businesses. It's still illegal for a company to fire a woman because she is pregnant (or even ask her during a job interview if her plans include child rearing), but the onus is on the wronged employee to prove discrimination.

Asking a potential employee if she plans on getting pregnant violates Title VII of the Civil Rights Act of 1964. But

BE BETTY

in order for that potential employee to prove that she was overlooked for a job based solely on her answer to that question, the potential employer would have to have admitted that he didn't hire her because he prefers to hire employees who will not be taking maternity leave in the near future. Good luck getting that on tape.

I do know a woman—a friend of a friend—who interviewed for a job with a nonprofit government agency. During the interview they not only asked about her familial intentions, but also committed an embarrassing faux pas by assuming she was currently pregnant. They asked if she planned to take maternity leave after her baby was born. Her baby had been born seven months prior and her husband was a stay-at-home dad, which is information they could have procured by asking the right (and legal) questions. Instead they assumed her leftover "baby weight" was real baby, insulted her in the process, and violated her rights by asking about her intention to take time off. Not only did the company lose a potential stellar and highly skilled employee, but it also found itself on the losing end of a potential lawsuit. The woman did file a complaint with the EEOC, and the matter was settled out of court for an undisclosed amount.

Less than one hundred years ago, women endured jail time, public scorn, and physical violence for standing up for their rights. Can you spare a few words of candor or a one-hour lunch meeting for yours? At the least, continue through the end of this book. Even if you walk away armed with one thing—ammunition to ask for that raise, the nerve to change your own title, or just a change in perspective ("It's just a job ... it's just a job")—it's worth the cover price.

WHAT YOU CAN DO:

✳ Lawsuits aren't the only way to get the attention of companies who discriminate against women. Anyone can file a complaint with the U.S. Equal Opportunity Employment Commission (EEOC). If you call (800) 669-4000, you will be referred to an EEOC field office in your area. The field office will interview you and determine if a charge should be filed. There is no cost to you for filing a charge. The EEOC is responsible for investigating all charges filed.

✳ Unfortunately, there is no method of obtaining a company's history of EEOC charges. The only person who has access to EEOC records for a company is the company owner.

✳ You can get answers to frequently asked questions at www.eeoc.gov.

IT'S NOT YOU,
IT'S YOUR WORK ENVIRONMENT

Being a Good Feminist doesn't mean being the Supreme Authority of All Things Politically Correct. It does mean that you might be the only one in the office with the guts to point out that office lunches at Hooters make women in the office uncomfortable. It doesn't have to involve a lawsuit, or even public embarrassment. In my experience most of these issues arise from ignorance, not maliciousness. And even when they are malicious, education can be your best defense.

Memorize the phrase "hostile work environment" and learn when to use it. Many people believe that discrimination has to be overtly hostile in order to be considered harassment. It doesn't, but it does have to fall under the U.S. Equal Employment Opportunity Commission's guidelines as to what constitutes harassment.

Reactionary behavior won't win you any allies. If you overreact anytime you're offended in the workplace, you're going to either be phased out (laid off, ignored, or even fired), or you'll be the one who's creating the hostile work environment. Hyper vigilance can backfire. It's important to know the law.

At a cocktail party a few years ago, after the subject of women and work came up, a very entertaining acquaintance regaled a group of us with stories about her current workplace and its myriad "violations" with regard to women's rights. There was the story about the coed bathroom and her discomfort about sharing such a private place with male coworkers (the bathroom was a single—not the stall variety), the story about the male intern who had a Jessica Alba screensaver (Was she clothed? Scantily, but yes, she was.), the story about the boss who added "making coffee" to the list of responsibilities for the female receptionist, and so on. The woman added that she had basically launched a one-woman crusade (because the other women in the office, according to her, couldn't be bothered to fight for their own rights) to end these injustices. Unfortunately none of the above behavior is illegal, nor does it violate Equal Employment Opportunity laws. What this woman described was typical of small businesses. A single coed bathroom for a company with eight employees is not unreasonable, unless the bathroom walls were papered with spreads from girly magazines. A screensaver of a woman in a bikini might be objectionable, but it isn't against the law. (Nude photos create a hostile work environment; other photos do not.) And, in a small office, asking the receptionist to make coffee isn't out of the ordinary. If her boss had asked the only female in a group of sales reps to take on the task of making coffee in the mornings simply because she was a female sales rep—that would violate EEOC guidelines.

Out of curiosity I asked the woman what her one-woman crusade involved. She had spoken to her boss on several occasions, frequently using the phrase "hostile work environment." She requested a women-only restroom (out of eight employees, three were women). She wanted the intern who had the Jessica Alba screensaver fired. She wanted her boss to make his own coffee. Unreasonable? Not exactly. I then asked her what she believed her status was at work—if she expected promotions, how the other employees responded to her, and so on. She said that most of her coworkers had distanced themselves, and she felt like her boss was looking for an excuse to fire her. "But I'm fine with that," she said. "I'm used to being the only bitch in the room. I'm the only woman who speaks up." Had she contacted the EEOC to report what she so strongly felt was discriminatory behavior? No. Instead she operated on high alert—hyper vigilant to any perceived wrong committed by her male co-workers—and turned every "incident" into a full-blown war.

SHE SPENT SO MUCH TIME POLICING THE ACTION OF OTHERS THAT SHE SCARCELY HAD TIME FOR ACTUAL WORK.

HER COWORKERS DISTANCED THEMSELVES BECAUSE THEY DIDN'T WANT TO BE BROUGHT INTO THE MELEE.

Of course her boss was looking for an opportunity to get rid of her. She spent so much time policing the action of others that she scarcely had time for actual work. Her coworkers distanced themselves because they didn't want to be brought into the melee. And if she wasn't careful, she'd end up the one making coffee after being demoted to receptionist.

The bottom line: She wasn't making less money than her male colleagues. No one was asking her to take clients to strip clubs. Her salary depended on commission, and she was given the same number of accounts as her male counterparts. She made less money because she spent less time in the field and more time "in meetings" with her beleaguered boss. Honestly, by the time she was done telling her story, I felt sorry for her boss. I've worked with women like this before, women who complain about getting a dumb blonde joke e-mail forward from a male coworker, but who thought nothing of forwarding e-mails about why dogs are better than men.

Fighting discrimination in the workplace requires dignity and restraint. We are women; we are not spider monkeys. If we run about screeching "foul" every time something offends us, we are not going to be taken seriously when there actually is something worth fighting for, such as not getting promoted because of our gender or being paid less than a living wage because the man signing the checks assumes our husbands are paying the lion's share of our household expenses and that our income is "extra." Fighting discrimination in the workplace doesn't mean that we want more privileges than men. We just want the same opportunities. The key word here is equal, and we should treat them the way we expect to be treated. Focusing more on whether or not you bring home the same size paycheck is more important than whether or not someone ignores basic rules of e-mail etiquette.

Rather than asking you to read page after page of the legalese that makes up the Federal Equal Employment Opportunity laws (my eyes roll back in my head just hearing that phrase), the EEOC was kind enough to sum it up in a readable format.

Familiarize yourself with these items so you can recognize whether or not a boss or coworker's behavior calls for action, or if it just pisses you off.

DEFINING HARASSMENT IN THE WORKPLACE

Unlawful harassment is a form of discrimination that violates Title VII of the Civil Rights Act of 1964 and other Federal authority.

(U.S. Equal Employment Opportunity Commission)

Unwelcome verbal or physical conduct based on race, color, religion, sex (whether or not of a sexual nature and including same-gender harassment and gender-identity harassment), national origin, age (forty and over), disability (mental or physical), sexual orientation, or retaliation (sometimes collectively referred to as "legally protected characteristics") constitutes harassment when:

✳ The conduct is sufficiently severe or pervasive to create a hostile work environment; or

✳ A supervisor's harassing conduct results in a tangible change in an employee's employment status or benefits (for example, demotion, termination, failure to promote, and so on).

Hostile work environment harassment occurs when unwelcome comments or conduct based on sex, race, or other legally protected characteristics unreasonably interferes with an employee's work performance or creates an intimidating, hostile, or offensive work environment. Anyone in the workplace might commit this type of harassment—a management official, coworker, or nonemployee such as a contractor, vendor, or guest. The victim can be anyone affected by the conduct, not just the individual at whom the offensive conduct is directed.

MY EYES ARE UP HERE
AND MY NAME ISN'T "BABE"

Here are some examples of actions that may create sexual hostile environment harassment:

✳ Leering (i.e., staring in a sexually suggestive manner)

✳ Making offensive remarks about looks, clothing, body parts

✳ Touching in a way that may make an employee feel uncomfortable, such as patting, pinching, or intentional brushing against another's body

✳ Telling sexual or lewd jokes, hanging sexual posters, making sexual gestures, and so on

✳ Sending, forwarding, or soliciting sexually suggestive letters, notes, e-mails, or images

Other actions that may result in hostile environment harassment, but are nonsexual in nature, include the following:

✳ Use of racially derogatory words, phrases, epithets

✳ Demonstrations of a racial or ethnic nature such as a use of gestures, pictures, or drawings that would offend a particular racial or ethnic group

* Comments about an individual's skin color or other racial/ethnic characteristics

* Disparaging remarks about an individual's gender that are not sexual in nature

* Negative comments about an employee's religious beliefs (or lack of religious beliefs)

* The expression of negative stereotypes regarding an employee's birthplace or ancestry

* Negative comments regarding an employee's age when referring to employees aged forty and over

* Derogatory or intimidating references to an employee's mental or physical impairment

Harassment that results in tangible employment action occurs when a management official's harassing conduct results in some significant change in an employee's employment status (e.g., hiring, firing, promotion, failure to promote, demotion; formal discipline, such as suspension; or an undesirable reassignment, change in benefits, compensation decision, or work assignment). Only individuals with supervisory or managerial responsibility can commit this type of harassment.

A claim of harassment generally requires several elements, including the following:

* The complaining party must be a member of a statutorily protected class;

* S/he was subjected to unwelcome verbal or physical conduct related to his or her membership in that protected class;

* The unwelcome conduct complained of was based on his or her membership in that protected class;

＊ The unwelcome conduct affected a term or condition of employment and/or had the purpose or effect of unreasonably interfering with his or her work performance and/or creating an intimidating, hostile, or offensive work environment.

WHAT IS NOT HARASSMENT?

Federal law does not prohibit simple teasing, offhand comments, or isolated incidents that are not extremely serious. Rather the conduct must be so objectively offensive as to alter the conditions of the individual's employment. The conditions of employment are altered only if the harassment culminates in a tangible employment action or is sufficiently severe or pervasive to create a hostile work environment.

~ *Source: The U.S. Equal Employment Opportunity Commission*

HOW TO FIND YOUR OWN INNER-BETTY

Think the glass ceiling is a myth? It's not. And unless you have thirty years (which, as mentioned before, is how long it will take, according to Economic Policy Institute statistics) to wait for the wage gap to close, it's up to you to find your own "inner-Betty." You can be your own labor activist without filing a formal complaint.

Ask nicely. It might seem like this goes against everything we should believe in as Good Feminists. Why should we have to be nice? We should be taking to the streets, carrying signs, shouting slogans, and loudly subverting the dominant paradigm of male oppression, right? Wrong. When it comes to your own job, your paycheck, and your success as an individual, forcing your feminist message down the throat of any male who dared to cross the line of your real or perceived civil rights can be a mistake. Yes, we should be taking to the streets to protest a halt on an increase in the minimum wage and banding together as women to make our voices heard whenever there is a policy that impacts us as a whole. But we can make just as much of an impact by first assuming that issues in the workplace result from ignorance or a lack of education on gender politics. If you've somehow discovered that your male coworkers' salaries are higher than yours, filing a complaint with the EEOC before speaking to your boss is a mistake. The first thing the EEOC will ask when you do file a complaint is what steps you've taken to remedy the situation. You should be prepared to list, by date, each attempt you've made to inform your supervisor, boss, VP, or other person in charge of the discrepancy, along with their responses.

The upside to being agreeable: It is quite possible that your lower salary was an oversight, an error, or a misunderstanding, or that there's a good reason why your counterparts are receiving higher wages. If that is the case, one meeting with your boss can rectify the problem and boost your salary. Even if the fault lies with your boss intentionally paying you less because you are female (or because you have a husband, or because you don't have a family to support, or any of the hundreds of other reasons cited by employers for paying women less), it is most likely that a meeting to discuss the discrepancy rationally would result in both an explanation and a solution. People who discriminate based on gender aren't always doing so out of maliciousness. There are specific morals and standards imposed by society that are so deeply ingrained, oftentimes people don't even realize their own bias. A rational meeting may not only achieve your goal, it may also help educate your boss (without making specific accusations) about his possible bias.

The downside to reactionary behavior: If you find out your male counterparts are being paid more and your boss shows up to work the next day to find you in the parking lot with a picket sign proclaiming *Unfair!* and *Equal Pay for Equal Work,* chances are you'll be out of a job. It's wrong for an employer to pay women less than men for the same job, but your behavior often dictates the em-ployer's reaction. If we act like unsta-ble and unreasonable people, it only contributes to the stereotype men often use about women being overly emotional and less than rational. And you could get fired, spend months filling out paperwork to file a complaint, and still come out unemployed in the end.

> OFTENTIMES PEOPLE DON'T EVEN REALIZE THEIR OWN BIAS.

Personally I don't mind being labeled "Office Bitch," but I do want to keep my job and I do want to get paid a fair wage. When I worked in an office full of men, I honestly didn't care what they called me behind my back. The raises were regular and generous and, when I did have to call on my inner-bitch, I did so rationally and with decorum.

Choose your battles. * Like the Girl

Who Cried Wolf, if you start pointing fingers at every single per-ceived transgression, eventually no one will listen. It is impor-tant to prioritize. Your own paycheck should be first on the list. As far as titles go, they're nice to have, but I don't care what my business cards say as long as the wages I earn are fair and competitive. Whether or not I get pats on the back for performing well matters less than regular raises.

If you do work with males who habitually make derogatory comments about women, treating them like ignorant children oftentimes does the trick. I like to use humor to point out why their language is offensive, rather than running to my boss's office with tales of their behavior. Despite the fact that we are all adults at work, it doesn't take much to regress to playground behavior. The boys throw rocks, the girls tell on the boys, the boys throw more rocks. I once worked with a man who frequently made offhand comments about women in the office. I let most of them go, because I knew he was ignorant and that no one took him seriously. I also knew he'd hang himself eventually—and it didn't take as long as I thought. He was in customer service and was often on the receiving end of complaints from customers. One customer called to complain about the service she received from one of the female customer service reps. He followed the book, for the most part, apologizing on behalf of the company, the female rep, and the universe. Then he made a comment I'd heard him make in the office but never to a customer: "She was having a bad day," he said, referring to the female rep. "It's her time of the month."

Unfortunately for him the customer was not only female herself, but she was also an attorney—for the American Civil Liberties Union (ACLU). Whether or not she called herself a feminist, I do not know. What I do know is that she wrote a letter to our boss, followed up by a phone call that resulted in the termination of the un-PC male coworker. Problem solved.

USE HUMOR

DOCUMENT.

DOCUMENT

Document everything. Save every e-mail, take notes in meetings, keep a log of all efforts made. There are a few reasons for this. First, your perception of how you presented a situation may be vastly different from how your boss perceives it.

Example: You stop by his office to express your interest in handling the Sweet account ("Hey boss, how's the Sweet account going?"). He sees it as a casual inquiry about the Sweet account. You see it as a firm request to take on the account. When he gives the account to your coworker, you're fuming—but he's clueless. It's helpful to have a record to return to when you're wondering if your anger is justified. IF you had stopped by his office and specifically said, "I'd like to take on the Sweet account" and followed up with an e-mail asking, "Is there anything I can do to improve my chances of landing the Sweet account?," and *then* he gave the Sweet account to your coworker, you'd be justified. You would also have a dated history to begin a discussion with your boss, eliminating the opportunity for him to squirm out with an "I didn't realize you wanted that account," and you're rationally holding him accountable.

Second, if you do have to file a complaint with the EEOC, you will need dated and thorough accounts of all attempts made to settle the matter before taking the next step. Filing a formal complaint is typically a last resort.

DOCUMENT.

CHAPTER TWO

GIRL POWER: WHERE'S MINE?

Wondering why you're not getting ahead at work?

Or, if you're just entering the workforce, how can you improve your chances of
(1) getting the job you want and
(2) moving up the corporate ladder?

Why are you waiting for someone to put you in charge?

Changes often happen quite ορgαnically in the corporate world. If you sit around waiting for someone to hand you your power, you're going to spend a lot of time sitting around. One of the secrets to getting promoted is taking on challenges without being asked—you do the work, prove yourself, and then have leverage to get a raise or promotion.

I've often seen this happen with younger employees and interns: They show up on time, do the minimum amount of work they must do to get by, and then wonder why no one has presented them with a promotion or job offer on a silver platter. When I was a kid and dragged my feet (as children often do), my mother always said, "What are you waiting for? An engraved invitation?" Although annoying as hell, it was

What are you waiting for?

An engraved invitation?

supposed to be funny. Now whenever I'm in a situation that lacks forward momentum—particularly at work—I remember that an engraved invitation is unlikely to land in my sticky little hands. I'm the only one who can propel myself forward.

> Most people who are successful at work are successful for a reason. They work hard. They bring in new accounts. They made $2 million for the company last year. They are the "go to" person for just about everything. I've yet to meet any successful person in the business world who said they "lucked into" their job, or that the Career Fairy came along and rapped their forehead with a magic wand, or that they happened to be in the right place at the right time. Yes, luck can be a factor in one's success, but the business world isn't the lottery. You can't just sit back and cross your fingers, hoping that you picked the right combination of numbers to land yourself a windfall.

When I finally landed my **dream job,** I received cards and flowers and multiple congratulations from friends and well-wishers. I was surprised how many people said, "You're so *lucky.*" The first time I heard it, I wanted to respond with all the snark I could muster, "Lucky? I worked my *ass* off to get this job." Instead I just muttered "thanks" and moved on. They didn't get it. But you can.

I was still in college—and working full-time at a software company—when I discovered *skirt!* magazine. Before *skirt!* I didn't know that such a thing as the personal essay existed. In 1997 I was writing personal essays, but I called them "stories" and I wrote them in my journal. I also didn't know that you could write for a living, unless you were a famous novelist or poet. I thought all magazine writers lived in New York City in high-rises and wore sneakers with their current-season Prada suits as they walked busy city blocks to get to work. When I found *skirt!*, I also found the story of the founder and publisher (and then editor, office manager, copywriter, and head of sales) Nikki Hardin. I knew I had to meet her.

Right around the same time, our local women's center was holding its annual women's conference at Ashley Hall School in Charleston. Gloria Steinem was the keynote speaker. And Nikki Hardin was going to be there. She still doesn't believe me when I say that I forked over my $80-something to attend the conference to meet her and not Gloria, but that's the truth. Seeing Gloria was great, but my real mission was to meet Nikki. I even stole a glance at the registration list, found out which sessions she was registered for, and skipped out of mine to attend the morning session she was in.

The session was about women and their working styles. There was an exercise during which we split into groups and strategically planned to overthrow and undercut the other groups so that we could be the winners. I lucked into Nikki's group. As the women discussed whether or not omitting information was as unethical as blatantly lying, I realized

I'M THE only one WHO CAN *propel* MYSELF FORWARD.

what was going on. The exercise wasn't about winning; it was a demonstration of how women tend to lean toward partnerships and fair play in the workplace, even putting loyalty and friendship before business success. We had to lie, and no one wanted to do it. I volunteered. We won. Suddenly every other group in the room, every other woman with the exception of the five in my group, hated my guts. I remember Nikki saying, "I can't believe you did that!" And then she invited me to join her and a few others on the lawn for lunch.

I'm almost positive I talked her ear off about myself and my writing in between peppering her with questions about her magazine. Before lunch was over, she had extended what I know now was a polite invitation to submit at my leisure. What I heard was a direct call to action, and I responded accordingly. Within a week I had submitted two essays, had one accepted, and decided that I would one day work for *skirt!*

Fast forward almost two years. I graduated from college in May 1999. In October I resigned from my job at the software company. The day after I carried my box of six years' worth of personal items from my office to my car and drove away from that building for the last time, I called Nikki at her office and invited her to lunch.

Two things you should know: First, if I'd known then what I know now, I would have sent an e-mail. Second, my ignorance about how things worked in the publishing world worked to my advantage. I met Nikki at a sandwich place across the street from the magazine's office and pitched idea after idea to her in between bites of my salad. I told her I wanted to work for her, full-time. She explained that they couldn't afford to hire another staff member. At the time, *skirt!* only had one location (Charleston) and a small staff (two salespeople, one graphic designer, an office manager, and Nikki), and at that point she'd only published three of my essays.

MY IGNORANCE ABOUT HOW THINGS WORKED IN THE PUBLISHING WORLD WORKED TO MY ADVANTAGE.

Because I was accustomed to the corporate world of meetings and meta-meetings (meetings about meetings), I had arrived prepared with what could only be called a sales pitch for my writing services neatly typed out and bound in a folder. It contained a lot of ideas, but the main one was that I could be

I'd never miss a deadline.

the writer she could count on. I asked for more than the going rate the magazine was paying writers at the time. In return I promised to deliver one essay a month on whatever that month's theme was—on time, guaranteed. I also offered to take on any other freelance work—columns, interviews, profiles—anything she needed for a reasonable rate.

BUT WHAT I DID FROM THERE IS MORE IMPORTANT: I FOLLOWED THROUGH.

I'm fairly certain she agreed, but I don't remember actually giving her the opportunity to say yes or no. But what I did from there is more important: I followed through. In my sales pitch I promised that I'd never miss a deadline, that I'd deliver an essay a month prior to her deadline, and that I'd complete any other assignments on time come hell or high water. (I might have even actually said "hell or high water.") For the next few years, I wrote one, sometimes two, essays a month and e-mailed them before my deadline. Nikki didn't run every single one—every essay can't be a hit—but for the most part, my essays were in the magazine once a month from 1999 on. She also began offering assignments—a column on resources for women here, an interview and profile there—and I always (always!) delivered on time. The first time I missed a deadline for *skirt!* was in January 2003. On the day of my deadline, my grandmother died after being hospitalized for a week. I had a partial essay done, but it had been a bad week. I called Nikki from my cell phone in the waiting area down the hall from where my grandmother's body awaited transport to the funeral home.

"I need an extension. My essay isn't done." Yes, I was upset about my grandmother's death. Her illness had been sudden and unexpected. And there was the obituary my mother wanted me to write, the picking out of an urn, the arrangement of the memorial services—but I'd never missed a deadline.

"Are you serious? Don't worry about your essay! Of course you can send it later. You don't even have to write one this month." I'm sure she thought I was nuts, but as much as I wanted to not care about my deadline and just be with my family, it was still difficult for me to break my perfect record.

So I went on conducting the business of saying goodbye to my Nana, writing her obituary, speaking at her memorial service, and, of course, finishing my essay. Actually, I scrapped my initial piece, which I think was something about a conversation I overheard at the gym written in my typical sardonic voice, and I wrote a new one. It was the first time I'd written a sad essay, but I delivered it within my extension window.

My point is not that one should put work obligations before everything else, including family and friends. I didn't forgo grieving in order to finish the work I had to do. I made it part of my work and pushed through it. I didn't stop mourning—I still miss her terribly—but work has always been the most normal part of my life, and I didn't need time off. I needed to work.

IN ORDER TO FUNCTION I HAD TO HAVE SOMETHING TO WORK TOWARD.

In late 2003 Nikki told me that she was going to sell *skirt!* to a company that could take the magazine to the next level. She wanted to bring *skirt!* to other markets, and this company could help make that happen. What it meant for me was that there was a chance she could finally hire me as a full-time editor. At that time, while freelancing for *skirt!*, I was also working full-time as managing editor for a small local newspaper. My salary was adequate and supplemented by frequent checks for freelance articles. Nikki was worried that the new company wouldn't be able to match my salary. I didn't press the issue, but I did tell her I would be ready to make the move when they were ready to have me on board.

Not quite six months later, at an art gallery event, Nikki offered me a job as editor for *skirt!* I don't think I even took a breath before I said yes. I was elated. Two weeks later I was at my new desk in *skirt!*'s office, trying to figure out why I wasn't happier. It took about three months to figure out what the problem was: I had been working toward something for so long; it was my top goal on my "five-year plan," but I hadn't planned what would happen next. In order to function I had to have something to work toward. During my first performance review at the magazine, I told Nikki I wanted to be vice president—of *skirt!*, not the United States. She must have been taken aback— I would have been. Sometimes I feel like a giant ego walking around on two legs. But she didn't discourage me. She said something along the lines of, "We'll see . . ." and changed the subject. I felt better at having put it out there, and I had a new goal to add to my new five-year plan, which, along with "Be VP" and "Learn Everything About Magazine Publishing," also included "Write Book." My fear now is that my next list will include things like "Buy Arizona" and "Take Over World."

So I waited five years to get my dream job, but I wasn't sitting back and literally waiting. In the interim I freelanced for dozens of magazines, including *Parents* magazine, an online portal (since folded) called ChickClick.com, and a startup called *Flair* magazine that Hearst Magazines was launching that was headed up by a former editor of *Vogue,* who also became a mentor by e-mail for me. I used the time to research markets, to ask stupid questions (like, "What does *graf* mean?" It's shorthand for paragraph, in case you're interested), and write for newspapers, something I'd never done before. When I pitched some story ideas to a local business newspaper, its editor asked me if I'd be interested in a part-time copyediting job. I wasn't sure what a copy editor did, but when you're a freelancer who has to pay rent, you don't turn down work. I knew there was a book or Web site out there somewhere that would tell me what to do, and I said, "Sure, I'll take it." Copyediting (which usually involves proofreading, editing for grammar and consistency, and fact-checking, in case you're interested) for the newspaper ten hours a week turned into working twenty hours a week as the newspaper editor, then into working forty-plus hours a week as managing editor.

An aside here: The fellow who hired me as part-time copy editor was a giant pain in the ass. He was in his seventies, a grizzly old ex-military newspaper journalist who wasn't smart enough to hide his misogyny. He even told me that he didn't like to hire female writers because "they aren't serious." At the time, I was platinum blonde, had a nose ring, and showed up for our initial meeting wearing knee-high leather boots and a pink miniskirt. Seeing his war memorabilia all over his office, I told him my father had been a "lifer" in the Navy. "What does your daddy do now?" he asked. My response: "I have no idea; we haven't spoken in eight years." He hired me anyway, without checking references or even asking if I had a college degree (I have two of them).

By the end of my first ten-hour week on the job, I hated him. I hated the way he printed out e-mails and wrote his responses on them before leaving them in a pile on my chair. I assumed he didn't understand how e-mail worked and, having worked for a software company, tried to educate him. He finally did start to respond to e-mails via e-mail, but DID SO IN CAPS EVERY SINGLE FREAKING TIME. Now he drove everyone crazy.

He asked me to sit in on story idea meetings with the rest of the staff, and he shot down every idea I had. He told endless stories about his military career. He was obtuse and derisive. He told me my skirts were too short. (They weren't, unless you're a seventy-year-old, right-wing, Republican white male). He made fun of the essays I wrote for *skirt!* (Why he read them, I still don't know.) During my second week at the newspaper, I went out for a beer with one of the staff writers. We bonded over our mutual hatred of the executive editor. He said, "I really don't know how long I can deal with this," and I asked him if anyone had done anything about it. "No," he said. "Everyone hates him but our publisher hired him, so there must be something good about him." Wrong. The publisher hired him, but he had no idea that our editor was so clueless. "What can you do?" shrugged my staff writer friend.

"I'll tell you what I can do," I said, fueled by three Guinness beers and a hatred of condescending men. "I'll have his job." My friend laughed. "I'd like to see that."

Two months later, the editor was fired and they offered me his job.

I know what you're thinking. Did I manipulate, wheedle, cajole, or otherwise act vengefully in order to advance my own personal agenda? *No, I didn't.* I didn't have to. I knew this man. One just like him lived in my house until I was eleven. I knew I could take him on, and I didn't have to use unethical means to get what I wanted. I could have taken it up with the publisher, but having worked for the company only a short time, I didn't know if my complaints would be seen as criticism of their decision to hire this man. I trust my own instincts, and they were telling me that it was a matter of time before he did himself in. In the meantime I decided that I was going to learn everything he knew about running a newspaper while he was still running one. **I became his right-hand woman.** I knew he was lazy and preferred to work half days so he could golf in the afternoon, so I asked him to show me how to do the things he didn't have time to do— which was everything. I have to add here that I attempted to explain why having a World War II Navy recruiting poster that read, "Gee! I wish I were a man …I'd join the Navy" was inappropriate; why responding to e-mails in all capital letters was received as if he were shouting; and why refusing to cover important business issues relating to women was a mistake (women business owners made up more than 50 percent of that newspaper's readership, something I learned simply by asking the circulation manager for demographic information).

The first time I challenged him in a staff meeting, I thought he was going to explode. He pitched the idea of having an issue dedicated to "women in business," and I said what I thought: Women won't respond to "Look at how cute these businesswomen are." Women should be included as part of the regular coverage—period. He basically told me to shut up.

My editor's behavior had always been erratic. In one breath he'd tell me how much he loved the newspaper business and in the next complain that he was too old to be working as much as he was (which was about twenty hours a week at that point). I didn't disagree. He butted heads often with the sales staff; I stood by waiting to smooth things over.

I didn't get him fired. He did himself in by accidentally forwarding an e-mail in which he'd scornfully referred to another employee as "stupid and lazy" to the entire staff, including the employee he was referencing. But technically, I guess I did show him how to use e-mail in the first place. Game, set, and match.

I spent the next two years learning how to manage a newspaper, while I managed a newspaper. Instead of waiting patiently in the wings for the Career Fairy to flutter down and appoint me managing editor, I made sure the publisher knew that I knew how to do my predecessor's job. *Some people might call it luck. I call it working my ass off.*

TO ME DIFFICULT PEOPLE ARE THE ONES WHO MAKE ME BETTER AT WHAT I DO.

Here's where you and I may differ: I love a challenge. *I can't function without one.* To me difficult people are the ones who make me better at what I do. They're critical, sometimes inappropriate, and have an uncanny ability to throw me off track.

Over the years I've developed a certain fondness for people like my former newspaper editor because they keep me on my toes and motivate me to work harder. If you have designs on the corner office and plan on working your way up the corporate ladder, but lack the ovaries to face these people head-on, you'd better find the courage and stamina, or get out of the game—because it is a game, and nothing you do or say is going to change that. If your primary goal is to make everyone at work like you, forget about management. Even if you do score the title, you won't be good at it.

Someone once asked me if I had my choice, would I work for a male boss or a female boss. I don't have a good answer for that. I've had a number of difficult bosses, some male, some female. I don't think gender was a factor in their level of difficulty. One thing they all had in common is that they had stopped listening to anyone who didn't sign their paycheck. I've had bosses who were terrible about delegating, who avoided confrontation, and who would rather submit to ritual torture than give someone feedback about their performance. However, they were good managers because they were tuned in to what was going on in the office—they genuinely listened. And they hired people (like me) who could help them delegate, confront, and give feedback.

TIP: ACTING LIKE THE BOSS YOU WANT TO WORK FOR IS THE BEST ADVICE I CAN GIVE YOU FOR WORKING YOUR WAY UP. NOT ONLY ARE YOU SETTING AN EXAMPLE FOR YOUR OWN BOSS, BUT YOU'RE ALSO GIVING COWORKERS AN IDEA OF WHAT YOU'D BE LIKE AS A BOSS. NOT THAT THE WORKPLACE OPERATES LIKE "AMERICAN IDOL," BUT THE POPULAR VOTE CAN GIVE YOU A HAND UP WHEN THE PROMOTIONS ARE BEING HANDED OUT.

EIGHT TIPS FOR GETTING AHEAD AT WORK

Control your temper. Assertiveness and tantrums do not go hand in hand. In fact, having a tantrum at the office is the fastest way to ensure that your boss and coworkers won't take you seriously. We all have tricks to keep our anger in check—figure out what works for you and use it.

Love change. Don't just expect it; greet it with hearty applause. Change is good. It's a lot easier to get ahead if you move forward on a wave of growth, and companies that resist change don't grow. You'll also stand out from the crowd, because most people react to change with fear and resistance.

Listen, don't talk. This doesn't mean you have to be the creepy, quiet one in the office. But take note of how often your superiors engage in personal chit-chat. If it happens often, rest assured that it will just be a matter of time before Chatty Cathy is on her way out and inscrutable you gets *her* job.

Shoot for perfection. Even if you're having a bad day, don't turn in half-finished or half-assed work. There are so many substandard chair warmers out there; you don't even have to exert *that* much effort to be perfect. Spell-check everything, even casual e-mails. Double-check facts and figures. Know your deadlines. Ask for help or advice. Don't rush through something just to get out the door by 5:00 p.m.

Be your own measure. Don't use your coworkers as a gauge for your success. Even if everyone else in the office spends afternoons surfing the 'net for pleasure or phoning contractors for their new kitchen, don't do it. You'd be surprised who's watching and listening, and you'll stand out if you're the productive one.

GIRL POWER: WHERE'S MINE?

TIPS continue ➢

Dress the part. You don't have to spend a million to look like you did if you're a smart shopper. Even if the workplace is creative-casual and your boss dresses down, you can still get a lot of mileage out of looking professional. Being professional just means being pulled together—not power suits and panty hose. You can express your individuality and still look "office-appropriate."

Lead before you are asked. Don't wait for a promotion to start taking on new challenges. Do your job, but keep one eye peeled for learning opportunities. Just because you've never used a software program or written a press release doesn't mean you can't figure it out. (Every software program has a help file, and you can find examples of press releases by Googling "press release").

Don't watch the clock. Even if this is JUST a job and you're going to write the next great American novel next year, treat every job like it's a career. As someone who has fired—I mean worked with—several employees who ran off like a shot as soon as the second hand lined up with the twelve at 5:00, I can tell you that your boss will notice that you'd rather be anywhere else.

STARTING FROM SCRATCH

Whether you're a recent college graduate, in college and trying to decide on your career path, unhappy with your current job and wanting to explore your options, or out of work and searching, there are several things you can do to give yourself the edge in a competitive job market.

Interview potential employers. No matter how badly you need the job, you should treat every job interview as if you were interviewing them, rather than vice versa. First, having as many questions for your interviewers as they have for you shows that you've done your research—something most employers look for in potential employees. Second, you will set up your own expectations and make your future employer aware of them from the very beginning by asking questions about whether or not raises are merit or seniority-based (let's hope the answer is "merit-based"), what the benefit package consists of, how often performance reviews occur, and what the company culture is. As early as the first interview with a company, it works to your advantage to make your prospective employer aware that your expectations for them are as high as the expectations they may have for you.

Treat internships like a paying job. I've had a lot of interns in my career, and I've seen it happen over and over again: The intern who seemed thrilled about working with me for a semester suddenly turns into the Invisible Woman after the internship is offered. I've had interns show up late or not at all, arrive at the office dressed for work, spend the few hours they've deigned to work discussing with anyone in earshot their weekend and how many Jägermeister shots they drank, call five minutes before meetings with flimsy excuses, call in sick more often than show up for work, and so on. I'm always surprised when an intern is shocked at being fired. I know her astonishment stems from the fact that she is working for free, so why should I care if she shows up on time? Here's why I care: Taking on an intern involves using my time to educate and train her so she is able to carry out her internship and learn about our business. When an intern shows up late or not at

The intern who seemed thrilled about working with me for a semester suddenly turns into the   after the internship is offered.

all, it's clear to me that she does not respect my time (or the company, or the internship). I've even had to fire interns who applied for our internship more than once, interviewed, and pulled every string available to get their foot in our door. However, once hired, they blew it. I know internships look good on résumés, but one should also keep in mind that they are also invaluable training opportunities, as well as potential semester-long job interviews.

When I ran a newspaper, I once had an intern who did every single thing right. She showed up on time, was enthusiastic, made it clear she wanted to learn everything about the business of journalism, and even took work home with her over school breaks. She

constantly asked what more she could do or learn or help. There were other interns during the semesters she worked, but none matched her level of professionalism or ability—and she knew it. Halfway into her first semester with us, she informed me that she wanted my job (or one like it). The following semester, rather than asking her back as an intern, I hired her as a part-time employee. While still taking a full course load, she threw herself into the job. Her favorite phrase to throw at me (from the movie *Working Girl*) was, "I'm right on top of that, Kel." Soon, before she'd even graduated from college, she was in charge of our internship programs (hiring to firing) and filling in for me when I was out of the office. One of the other editors and I came up with a nickname for our high-performing former-intern-turned-editorial-assistant: "Hostile

Takeover." The "hostile" part was a joke, but the takeover part wasn't. I was promoted to managing editor only because she was there, upon college graduation, to step into my shoes full-time as assistant editor. She became so invaluable to me in my own job that when I left the newspaper to work for *skirt!*, I knew I'd find a way to bring her along eventually. It took a few months, but "Hostile Takeover" is now one of *skirt!*'s editors—and she says it is her "dream job."

HOSTILE
TAKEOVER

Right place, right time? Wrong. She worked her tail off, was creative and outspoken and assertive. She knew how to read people, and she understood what I needed from her without me having to ask. And that was just as an unpaid intern. By throwing herself into that job from day one, she created the foundation for a future in the field of her choice. Even if she had moved on to work elsewhere, the fact that she took it upon herself to learn everything she could about the newspaper and publishing business meant that she could do that anywhere, in any job she chose to pursue. I'm glad she stuck with us.

Make negotiating a priority. Just because you're fresh out of college with little or no experience doesn't mean you don't have ground to stand on when it comes to negotiating a competitive salary *(see Chapter 7: Mind the Gap and Settling Up)*. Part of your research before applying for a job should be visiting sites like Salary.com or Monster.com to find out the position's pay range. Both sites have salary calculators broken down by field, region, and company size. Because your potential employer has the advantage if you don't even have a range in mind, being prepared has the added bonus of showing your potential employer that you have the competence to negotiate—a key ability in most career fields. As a hiring manager, I am always impressed when a candidate interviews for a job and has an answer for what salary range she expects. When someone answers with an "I don't know," or if she throws the question back at me, I assume she either hasn't done her homework, or she doesn't care enough to ask for a competitive salary. Either way, that's not someone I want working for me. I'd much rather see a candidate ask for more than we're offering so that I have a starting point to negotiate on my company's behalf.

Demonstrate enthusiasm. Nothing is worse than interviewing a candidate who seems like she couldn't care less about getting the job. If you're interviewing with a company, you should have researched the company thoroughly and, if you go through with the interview, it should be because there's something about that company that appeals to you as an employee. Share this with your interviewers. Tell them what you like about their company, why you decided to interview with them, why you're interested in the job, and what you think you can do for them. Don't make them drag the information out of you. If they have to do it and hire you anyway, they get what they deserve—an unenthusiastic, lukewarm, mediocre employee. Don't be that.

Onward!

CHAPTER THREE

PLAYING NICE: ALPHA AND BETA ARCHETYPES AT WORK

In Western civilization, the historical feminine archetype has always been a passive woman. The stand-by-your-man, Mrs. Myhusband's Name, we-don't-want-to-rock-the-boat kind of female. However, as I sit here some forty years after the birth of the women's movement I missed out on, I realize that there's a new archetype in town.

And she's pissed.

The first alpha female of whom I was aware was my grand-mother. The second was Gloria Steinem, American feminist icon and founder of *Ms. Magazine*. Nana started the first seamstress union in Massachusetts long before there was any such regulation in female-dominated professions. She was the one who told me that loudmouthed women were once burned at the stake as witches. "They don't do it anymore," she added conspiratorially. I took it as a go-ahead.

I remember my mother talking about Gloria Steinem and *Ms. Magazine* over fondue with the other officers' wives who were probably more familiar with Gloria Vanderbilt and *Good Housekeeping*. I have three sisters and no brothers, so in my house the women outnumbered the men. But even if that hadn't been the case, I suspect my mother would have ruled the roost anyway. My father, a military man who spent months at a time at sea, was rarely present (who could blame him?), but tended to assert his power through fear rather than benevolent authority. And he was gone before I reached high school, so my alpha mother's influence won out nonetheless. In fact, it may have been my mother's drive to have a career outside of and in addition to raising four girls, combined with her giving dear old Dad the boot when she discovered he was having an affair, that set my own course for independence. I knew two things: I wanted a successful career, and I never wanted to be in a situation where I had to choose between financial security or leaving a man.

I'VE BEEN CALLED ANY NUMBER OF THE FOLLOWING

CONTROL FREAK PUSHY CONFIDENT

B I T C H

Because of the alpha traits I inherited/acquired—leaving jobs and men who didn't respect me, insisting on consideration both at work and at home—over the years I've been called any number of the following: Control freak. Pushy. Confident. Aggressive. Forceful. Dominant. Hyperambitious. Disagreeable. Bitch. In my mind, it just meant that I wanted more than what I was handed, always more than what I had. And I didn't mind the name-calling; I would have been happy to have any one of the above printed on a business card in lieu of a title (and a former boss once actually had "Head Bitch" cards printed for me as a gift, complete with company logo. I adored them).

I assumed any female who didn't have alpha traits had simply chosen the path of least resistance. It has to be easier, I reasoned, to be agreeable and complacent than contrary and outspoken. Even in grade school I somehow managed to wrangle myself into leadership positions. Most of the time I wasn't even sure how it happened, other than I was often the first to speak up and my voice was often the loudest.

In most of the jobs I have had, I started out with a modest objective: make enough money to support myself. I started off waiting tables during my first year of college—but then somehow ended up managing the restaurant. I thought I could handle it all, but soon I had to resign as my grades strained under the weight of a fifty-hour-a-week job on top of a full class schedule. I next took an entry-level job as a file clerk for a software company, intending to spend my days mindlessly alphabetizing and making copies, which would free up my brain to think brilliant thoughts and focus on school. However, within three years I was not yet a college graduate but was managing a staff of twenty-plus employees. Post-college and after a few years of freelancing, I took a less-than-part-time job copyediting for a newspaper in order to have some modest regular income to supplement my sporadic checks for writing. Within a year I was managing editor for that newspaper. I guess you could say I always fell into a leadership role, even if it wasn't intentional.

I learned a lot, but often wondered if sticking to my original role (in any of these jobs) would have changed anything for me. Focusing on my career instead of relationships, never being satisfied with the status quo, pushing myself into sixty-hour workweeks, taking on and taking on and taking on— what was I trying to prove?

I thought beta females allowed their need to be liked to override their ambitious tendencies. But, as it turns out, I was the one seeking validation, approval, and admiration. I was not a Caring Nurturer. I thought that my achievement was worth more because I had to struggle more to get there. I thought I

I THOUGHT THAT MY ACHIEVEMENT WAS WORTH MORE BECAUSE I HAD TO STRUGGLE MORE TO GET THERE.

had to get angry to create momentum. Passivity was the enemy, and I wasn't going to let it lead me astray. But with maturity came some semblance of clarity. I discovered that I didn't have to run everyone else off the road to get to the finish line. In fact I'd missed out on a lot of opportunities by dismissing some of the beta females who probably could have taught me a thing or two—like how to shut my mouth and listen to other people and how to play well with others—and perhaps even inspire a dash or two of humility.

And somewhere along the way, I learned to stop resenting people for not being like me. After personally turning a few workplaces into battlefields, making more than one assistant or intern cry, and being bitter as hell about always having to be the bitch in the boardroom, I learned that not every woman has alpha qualities. If all women did, we'd probably live in a Mad Max Beyond the Thunderdome world, with roving packs of dominant females battling it out to be Queen of the Hill.

As with any other subjugated group in history, the biggest menace to the success of the alpha female is the alpha female herself. There are so many of us, yet we split into factions, fight one another, and generally make things difficult—particularly in the workplace, but also at Mommy & Me, book clubs, philanthropic boards, and any guild, organization, or group with more than two members.

The new alpha female is more hybrid than harpy. She's benevolent (Melinda Gates, Oprah Winfrey), powerful (Martha

Stewart, Anna Wintour), eloquent (Maya Angelou), sweet (Katie Couric), sexy (Sharon Stone), informed (Maureen Dowd), and savvy (Sallie Krawcheck).

In order to take over the world, we must learn from the mistakes of the alpha males that preceded us. They're arrogant (Donald Trump), sordid (Lars Bildman, former president and CEO of Astra USA, who was "relieved of his responsibilities" after an investigation into rampant long-term sexual harassment), dishonest (Michael Kopper, ex-Enron executive), fraudulent (Halliburton), discriminatory (too many male CEOs to list here), greedy (ex-Tyco CEO Dennis Koslowski), and blowhards (Rush Limbaugh). Backstabbing and manipulation might have worked for them for a time, but the fact that we managed to slip in while they were taking swings at each other should tell us something.

If it comes down to only two choices—fighting with the other alphas or dismissing the betas—there can only be one winner. But if we take the time to work with alphas rather than against them and realize there is much to be learned about compassion and temperance from the betas, we really can create an altruistic workplace.

PLAYING NICE

Until recently, being the alpha that I am, I didn't think I was crossing a line by calling a beta a beta. I was in a meeting with several women who were discussing the office politics of their particular workplace (which was not mine). One of the women complained ad nauseam about a coworker (who was not present). The coworker, according to this woman, "just did whatever she wanted." She "didn't care about anyone else's feelings." She was "only out for herself." She was also the top sales producer in the office. "I think you have yourself an alpha there," I told the coworker, who, because she'd never taken this woman on, or complained about her to management, or tried to assert herself, was clearly a beta.

"WHAT DO YOU MEAN, 'ALPHA'?" asked the beta,

and I explained that there were generally two types of people: alphas and betas (see Archetypes Defined on page 51).

In a wolf pack, the alpha female is usually the strongest, wisest, and oldest member of the group. She's a good hunter and decision maker and gets to mate with the alpha male. Humans are pack animals, just like wolves, and also follow a sort of social pecking order. The human alpha female (sometimes referred to as "Queen Bee" or "Mean Girl") is the individual in her given community (a workplace, for example) the others follow and defer to. Betas . . . well, to me, betas are everyone else.

Alphas are mavericks, are outspoken, appear fearless, focus on goals and achievements, and tend to be less sensitive than their beta counterparts. On a good day, alphas run companies. On a bad day, they make a lot of enemies.

> HUMANS ARE PACK ANIMALS, JUST LIKE WOLVES, AND ALSO FOLLOW A SORT OF SOCIAL PECKING ORDER.

Betas, on the other hand, prefer to work as part of a group toward a common goal. They see their role as that of the supporter, rather than trailblazer—but important just the same. They are compassionate, nurturing, and sensitive to nonverbal signals like facial expression and body language. They are loyal employees. They are also nonconfrontational, soft-spoken, and sometimes passive-aggressive (often referred to as the "Danger

Beta"). On a good day, betas make the office a happy place to work. On a bad day, betas cry at their desks.

"So what am I?" asked the beta. I'm a terrible liar, especially when the only benefit is to spare someone's feelings, so I told her. She didn't take it as well as you'd think, and—with tears in her eyes—proceeded to rattle off three reasons why she was not a beta female, complete with examples from college. Unfortunately the only one I can recall was something about cheerleading and her sorority, because my brain was busy through the rest of her speech relegating her to gamma girl. "You're right," I said. "You're not a beta," adding silently to myself, *because a beta would eat you for breakfast.*

DANGER BETA

The moral of this story: There's always someone willing to keep her mouth shut to avoid making waves. The alpha in this story got her way time and time again because the beta never stood up to her, not even a peep. If you're a beta and you've never stood up to an alpha, the first time can be daunting. But once an

ONCE AN ALPHA REALIZES THAT YOU WON'T ALLOW YOURSELF TO BE BULLIED, YOU'LL GAIN HER RESPECT— WHETHER SHE LIKES IT OR NOT.

alpha realizes that you won't allow yourself to be bullied, you'll gain her respect—whether she likes it or not. Try putting

yourself in uncomfortable situations outside of the workplace, like taking an improv class or an extension program public-speaking workshop. Chances are you won't be called upon to orate at length during a work meeting (or perform a stand-up comedy routine), but doing these things in a safe environment where your paycheck isn't at stake makes the small steps you can take at work that much easier.

YOU KNOW YOU'RE AN ALPHA WHEN:

✳ None of your coworkers will look you in the eye.

✳ You're the unofficial keynote speaker at most of your staff meetings.

✳ You feel like you could do anyone's job better than she does it, including the receptionist and the person who delivers sandwiches at lunch.

✳ You see a little doll on a coworker's desk that looks a bit like you, except it has pins stuck through it.

✳ You're working sixty-hour weeks because everyone else is incompetent.

✳ You haven't taken a vacation in years because the company would fall apart without you.

✳ You don't know what it feels like to be wrong.

✳ You've been called "intense" or "forceful" because everyone else is too nice to call you a bully or a bitch.

✳ You're the resident problem solver—from issues of corporate litigation to overflowing toilets.

IF YOU'RE AN ALPHA

If you're an alpha, remember that being dismissive and negative is bad news in the workplace. No matter where you fall in the chain of command, acting like the CEO you'd want to work for is always a better tactic than steamrolling your coworkers. Model yourself after the most successful person in your workplace or, if your workplace isn't chock-full of good examples, read biographies of women in business, like *Tough Choices: A Memoir* by former HP CEO Carly Fiorina, or *Elizabeth I, CEO: Strategic Lessons from the Leader Who Built an Empire* (yes, that's Queen Elizabeth) by Alan Axelrod.

> ACTING LIKE THE CEO YOU'D WANT TO WORK FOR IS ALWAYS A BETTER TACTIC THAN STEAMROLLING YOUR COWORKERS.

Try listening with interest instead of waiting for the other person to pause so you can cut them off. Your ideas might be the best, but when you stop listening to other people, eventually they will also be the only ideas you'll have to work with. Shutting people out is not only bad for morale, but it's bad for business.

Try getting behind someone else's idea, just once. You will always have to fight the impulse to interrupt and learn how to temper your impatience with tolerance. Besides, once you're the boss, you'll already have a handle on who the real stars in your office are.

Yes, you might be smarter and more competent than everyone else, but you just might be sabotaging yourself with your inflexibility. The only solution to your frequent complaints about no one else stepping up is to allow someone else to step up, so give her a hand when she does. Use your powers for good (recognizing that some of your behavior stems from fear and insecurity), and you won't feel like the workplace is a battlefield. A little generosity goes a long way, and sometimes it's as simple as asking how things are going—and then really listening to how things are going. Encourage and step back. Give a pep talk and step back. Offer advice and step back. Not only will you be contributing to the success of someone else, but you'll also be adding to your own by earning her gratitude. Women—especially beta women—are loyal by nature, and you just might find the backup you'll need down the road (and up that ladder).

YOU KNOW YOU'RE A BETA WHEN:

✽ You believe in a kinder, gentler workplace.

✽ You have good ideas; it's just that no one ever listens to them—or you.

✽ You've been stuck with the lunch order more times than you care to admit.

✽ Someone in the office has made you cry.

✽ When it's time for your review, you have trouble coming up with a list of your achievements, because you feel like you're bragging.

✽ You've ever left a job because someone was mean to you.

✽ You've baked cookies for the office.

✽ It's really important that you like your coworkers and that your coworkers like you.

IF YOU'RE A BETA

If you're a beta, don't let them push you around. When it comes down to fight or flight, you almost always choose the latter. But if you pick your battles wisely, trust your own judgment, and remember that an alpha's bark is always worse than her bite, you'll realize that standing your ground gets easier every time.

Try starting small. One-on-one meetings are a safer place to express yourself than staff or board meetings. Or if that's too much to start with, get a pushy nonwork friend to stand in for some role-playing practice sessions.

> BITCHING MIGHT MAKE YOU FEEL BETTER, BUT IT ISN'T A LONG-TERM SOLUTION.

Try speaking your mind. Being opinionated isn't a bad thing, and it doesn't mean you don't value what other people have to say. Timidity most often stems from a lack of confidence. Ask yourself: Do I really know what I'm talking about? Chances are you do. And it won't do you (or your company) any good to remain silent.

Try using your power where it matters. If you're unhappy at work, even if you're the beta-est beta in the world, someone knows about it. Your friend in accounting knows about your overtalker, credit taker of a colleague. Another coworker has heard all about your great ideas over cocktails; the problem is, she's not your boss and can't help you put them into action. Bitching might make you feel better, but it isn't a long-term solution. The most important thing is to stop bitching to people who can't change your situation and start doing something to change it yourself.

Because I am an alpha, I have a tendency to take charge when a crisis presents itself. I live my life in problem-solution mode: Problem? Solution. End of discussion. Sometimes I have to remind the betas around me that I *do* want to hear their ideas, and I am most often incredibly grateful when someone else speaks up, because it takes the pressure off. If you're a beta, stalling tactics work well to give you some time to get your thoughts in order and, if necessary, give yourself a little pep talk before jumping in feetfirst. My own beta mantra is, "I'm good at my job … I'm good at my job." I *am* good at my job; sometimes I just have to remind myself on days when my confidence wanes. Stalling tactics include these lines: "Let me just run back to my desk and get my notes on that," "I have to make a quick call; can we meet in the conference room in ten minutes?," and (my personal favorite, learned from my psychotherapist mother) "So what I hear you saying is that we have a serious problem with XYZ. Can you give me some background?" (and use that background summary time to gather your own thoughts).

Every beta has a tiny alpha inside—and vice versa. Let the little one out every now and then; you might be surprised at the results when your inner-alpha throws a little muscle around, or your inner-beta turns a volatile meeting into a problem-solving roundtable.

REVIEW YOURSELF

One of the best practical exercises for bringing out your inner-alpha is to review your own job performance before your official review time rolls around. Most companies have annual or biannual performance reviews or evaluations. Instead of waiting for your review time to roll around, keep a running list of what you've accomplished at work. Refer and add to it often. Set a weekly alarm reminder on your computer or make an appointment in your datebook to update the list. Not only will it help keep you on task, it also gives you license to sing your own praises when you don't have to worry about someone else reading it. In time, blowing your own horn becomes second nature. Ask yourself some sample questions, such as:

* What are the key strengths you bring to your job?

* Over the past year, what do you see as your most significant accomplishments to the goals of the office?

* What ideas or projects did you propose and/or initiate over the past year?

* What are your weaknesses or areas for improvement that you would like to work on next year?

* What have I accomplished over and above my job description?

> **TIP:** SEARCH GOOGLE FOR "SAMPLE PERFORMANCE REVIEW" TO GET MORE QUESTIONS AND IDEAS FOR SELF-EVALUATION.

ARCHETYPES DEFINED

Alpha: (adj.) In mammals, having the highest rank of its sex in a dominance hierarchy; being the most prominent, talented, or aggressive person in a group. Alpha females tend to possess negative traits such as an inflated sense of self-importance, inflexibility, and recklessness, as well as positive traits such as decisiveness, determination, and confidence.

Beta: (adj.) Second in order of importance; a less-aggressive female member of the pack. Often possessing a marked lack of self-confidence, anxiety, and the inability to make decisions. On the plus side, beta females are inclusive, loyal, and tend to work very well as part of a team.

Danger Beta: (n.) A passive-aggressive and hostile beta female, often an alpha disguised as a beta, using her powers to wreak havoc and chaos. This beta has a chip on her shoulder and therefore can be a nightmare to work for, should she manage to backstab her way to a corner office.

Gamma Girl: (n.) A need-to-pleaser; an easier-to-let-others-make-decisions kind of gal. Gammas often think they are betas, but they lack the survival instincts to create forward momentum in the workplace.

aggressive

CHAPTER FOUR

WORK LIKE A GIRL

You're a star.

You know it. Your mom knows it. Even your best friend knows it. So why doesn't your boss give you the recognition you deserve?

A better question to ask yourself is: *Why are you expecting recognition?*

During my first foray into the corporate world, I was still in college and young—maybe twenty-two years old. I was also naïve. As my work ethic dictated, I threw myself into the job. I was hired as a file clerk, but the company was growing and I knew I could do more than shuffle files in a job that required skills beyond knowing the alphabet. My need to please had me working late hours, teaching myself how to use the company's software programs, and picking up extra projects for my boss, who I had subconsciously placed into the role of parental authority figure. I waited for "good job" or any other sign that my efforts had been recognized. When it didn't come, I began to resent my boss for dumping work on me (never mind that I'd *asked* for the work). It wasn't until a few years later when I was in a management role with a staff of younger employees looking to *me* for recognition that I realized how I'd put myself in the position of repeating a role from childhood. I was raised in a single-parent household without male role models, and I found that I reenacted the role of attention and approval-seeker without even realizing I was doing it, particularly with male bosses.

I'm sure that men also find themselves in this situation, but it seems to be a trap that women fall into often. We replay roles from childhood throughout adulthood, putting our bosses in the role of parent and our coworkers in the role of siblings, and we basically set ourselves up for repeating these patterns on a subconscious level. In my case my resentment at not being recognized for working so hard manifested itself in the form of a sort of teenage rebellion. I refused to comply with various policies, including writing up members of my staff for what I thought were insignificant transgressions (like being late). And I got my nose pierced. It was the early 1990s, and nose rings weren't prevalent in mainstream society the way they are now. And it was a fairly conservative company. Out of a few hundred employees, fifty or so in management, I was the only employee—or manager—with a nose ring.

AS WOMEN OUR SELF-WORTH IS OFTEN TIED INTO WHAT WE DO FOR OTHER PEOPLE.

Granted, I didn't have to work face-to-face with clients (I ran a customer service call center), but I was expected to dress and present myself in a certain way. It sent my bosses into a tizzy, because neither the employee handbook nor my employment contract contained any language prohibiting facial jewelry. Nevertheless they wanted me to take it out. I refused and went back to work.

Whether or not you've done it yourself, you've probably seen this behavior in friends or coworkers. Some of us get tattoos. Some of us spend our water cooler time bitching about this boss or that one. Some of us spend time on the clock working on our novel, e-mailing college friends, or daydreaming about running away to build huts in Malaysia.

Despite my latent teenage rebellious attitude toward my bosses, I was even more committed to my job. And I was good at it. I got regular raises and took on more and more responsibility. My biggest mistake was not seeing my own value and realizing that, by paying me more money at regular intervals, the company *was* giving me the pat on the back I'd been resenting not having. The only thing that should have mattered is that I received raises and promotions based on merit. The raises were substantial, and I was a mid-level manager in my mid-twenties with two years of college left to finish. Why was I looking to my boss for encouragement?

As women our self-worth is often tied into what we do

I was also naïve.

for other people. We're nurturers by nature and expect the same nurturing in return. Men are raised to take criticism, and their self-worth is often tied into being providers. Had I taken the latter point of view rather than the former, it would have been enough for me to receive regular salary increases, and I wouldn't have reacted negatively to a lack of emotional validation. If this is you—if you don't see money as validation and find yourself wanting to be appreciated more than you want a larger paycheck—it's time to change. When little boys skin their knees, they're told to suck it up and walk it off. When little girls skin their knees,

WE'RE NURTURERS BY NATURE AND EXPECT THE SAME NURTURING IN RETURN.

don't thank me; pay me

we're allowed to run to a parent for comfort. Boys and men are often discouraged from nurturing others because it is not masculine or "macho" for men to show their nurturing side and skills. Young boys may get teased for playing with dolls or having a favorite teddy bear. I'm not suggesting that the solution is to act like men in the workplace (in fact I will repeat over and over again that we should not act like men in the workplace). What I am suggesting is that we make ourselves aware of our upbringing, environment, and the roles in which society places male and female children, consciously or otherwise. Nurturing is more a matter of personality and skills, not gender. Separating your emotional reactions from true validation is necessary. Forget about pats on the back and other warm and fuzzy forms of support. My mantra is, "Don't thank me; pay me."

THE BOTTOM LINE

Your boss is not a substitute parent. If you're expecting pats on the back or "Way to go, kiddo," you're going to be sorely disappointed. Business is business and, while you might enjoy the company of your boss and coworkers, your own misguided loyalty can be your worst enemy.

You have to have enough insight to understand your own psychological patterns in order to recognize and correct what's happening in your subconscious. The same traits that make women compassionate and intuitive managers of others can also set us up for failure when we mentally turn our bosses into parental figures.

THERE'S NO CRYING IN BASEBALL

Speaking of turning bosses into parental figures, another exasperating aspect for me was that I couldn't handle being yelled at by men. Before my parents divorced, my father was a volatile presence in the household. He had a bad temper and often went off on tirades. As a young adult any time a male raised his voice to me, I cried. In a work situation, I could control it on some level, but the added embarrassment and anger at myself for becoming tearful often exacerbated the situation and the tears. It didn't happen often, but it was often enough that I thought it was something I needed help to work on.

In my family, because my mother is a shrink, when we have something to work on, we do what we always do: see someone. In my early twenties, unhappy with my life, my job, my fifty-hour workweeks, and full course load in school, my stress level was maxed out. I decided to see a therapist for a year.

The reason I committed to going for a year would be familiar to anyone who grew up in the household of a shrink: We think we're immune to therapy, or at least, we think we're smarter than the therapist. I saw a shrink for the first time at age eleven, when my parents divorced. Like most eleven-year-olds, talking about my feelings and emotions was low on my list of priorities, even in an office packed with toys and games and finger paints. I spent most sessions clammed up and sitting cross-legged on his couch. It took six months, but my mother finally put an end to my misery and stopped the sessions.

I WILL REPEAT OVER AND OVER AGAIN THAT WE SHOULD NOT ACT LIKE MEN IN THE WORKPLACE.

In my late teens, I saw therapists for other reasons, but I always found a reason by the second or third month to stop.

This therapist brought up God every session. That one knew my mother professionally and probably reported back to her (probably not, but in my teenage mind . . .). Another just didn't like me—I could tell. Another never remembered anything I told her.

But now I knew my career and education were on the line, so I committed to seeing a therapist once a week for a year, whether I liked it or not. It was during that time, in those sessions, that I realized I was playing out my childhood dramas at work. The approval I wanted from my boss is the approval I didn't get from my father. The tears that came every time my boss criticized me harshly or raised his voice are the same tears from when my father used to yell at us. It was time to grow up.

Once I recognized the problem, it became easier to manage. My first response when someone raises his voice to me even now is to cry, but because I understand where it comes from, I am able to put some distance between my feelings and the problem at hand and not take the criticism personally. And I can control both the tears and my anger. Following this breakthrough I did see my therapy through and completed the year, and I think I came out the other side better for it. It was helpful to have someone who listened to my frustration but who wasn't involved. Women also have a habit of using their coworkers as de facto therapists. **Big mistake.** Getting your coworkers involved in your personal dramas not only leaves you exposed and relegates you to weakest member of the herd, it also drags them down with you.

There's no crying in baseball—or at work. It's perfectly natural to take criticism personally. Men do it; they just don't leak from the eyes. Once I found myself in the situation of having a crying employee in my office, I realized that it's just as uncomfortable for the cry-ee as it is for the crier.

Keep it to yourself and find an impartial third party—even if you have to pay them to do it.

THERAPY

Therapy doesn't have to be expensive. Most therapists will file a claim with your health insurance provider so that you're only responsible for the co-pay. If your insurance doesn't cover mental health claims at all (shame on them), there are therapists who work with clients on a sliding scale based on income and financial situation. If your company does cover mental health as part of its insurance plan, it probably also offers an Employee Assistance Program (EAP) that you can call for a referral to a local therapist covered under the plan.

"I want to work for a company that contributes to and is part of the community. I want something not just to invest in. I want something to BELIEVE *in."*

~ ANITA RODDICK, FOUNDER OF THE BODY SHOP

We are girls, we are females, we are women—but don't let other people take those things and turn them into reasons why we deserve less and why we should be considered weaker, lacking in intelligence, and run by our emotions. Women have many characteristics that make us natural leaders.

For instance, the very same nurturing instincts that can lead us astray on a career path by allowing us to become sidetracked looking for external validation are also the instincts that make us compassionate managers. A good manager understands that, while the bottom line comes first, they are still managing a function that involves human beings. Women are less likely to put that fact aside, and we are able to focus both on the bottom line and on individual members of our staff.

In management positions, I've always believed that I am not managing people; I am managing a function, and that function involves people. I don't even say, "This is so-and-so, she works *for* me." I say, "This is so-and-so, we work together." Micromanagement never works. A good manager hires people who are perfectly capable of managing themselves.

In hiring employees we're taught to rely on the facts and never our "gut reaction." However, it is difficult not to allow our instincts to factor into hiring decisions. Women tend to lean toward making instinctual decisions based on whether or not we get a good "vibe" or if we like someone. Men tend to make the more logical hiring decision based on the facts of a résumé, experience, background, and so on. I think a combination of the two can be channeled into smart hiring. I usually keep a mental checklist; if all the right qualifications are present, then I'll do a "gut check" and see how I feel about the candidate. If something just doesn't feel right, I'll dig a little deeper, ask more probing questions during an interview, and try to determine what's causing my trepidation.

Early in my career when I was initially hiring staff for my department at a software firm, I attended several seminars and workshops on hiring practices and legal issues, human resource training, and conferences on attracting employees. Just about every workshop I attended included a section on hiring against your instincts. Hiring decisions, according to these training sessions, should be made based on facts and not your gut. You

Micromanagement never works.

can't not hire someone just because you don't like them, and when I initially began interviewing and hiring employees, I ignored what my gut said. I made a lot of poor hiring choices.

> **TIP:** YOUR INSTINCTS HELP INFORM YOU ABOUT THINGS THAT ARE NOT PRESENT ON A CANDIDATE'S RÉSUMÉ, SUCH AS PERSONALITY TYPE AND HOW THEY WILL FIT IN WITH THE REST OF THE STAFF, POTENTIAL MENTAL INSTABILITY (YES, THAT HAPPENED), AND GENERAL NEGATIVITY.

No one (in her right mind) will be negative during a job interview. But with someone who has that tendency, it will crop up later, and it's one of the most difficult things to address with an employee. You can sit down and have a progress meeting with a staff member and outline specific goals, such as "learn XYZ software" and "make forty outgoing calls per day." You cannot sit down and overhaul someone's basic personality. One negative person (just one!) can bring a whole team down. I hope you're not that person, but even more, I hope you don't hire her.

It took me a long time to find the right balance, and I haven't always made stellar hiring decisions (it would be impossible to predict the future), but I have been comfortable with what I base my decision on.

1 negative person

WORK LIKE A GIRL

(just one!)
can bring a whole team down.
I hope you're not that person,
but even more,
I hope you don't hire her.

THE TIMES ARE A-CHANGIN', RIGHT?

One myth I've heard time and time again in relation to female CEOs (and other positions of power, such as president of the United States) is that women are "too emotional" to make important decisions when millions of dollars are at stake. As if we'd have a surge in hormones and start selling off the high-yield stock, or blow a deal because we just watched Oprah and feel too teary to think about stupid things like contracts and dollars. Men make decisions with their emotions, too—emotions are not gender specific. Certainly, as I mentioned before, women are not raised to stuff our feelings back down. Little girls are allowed to cry, while little boys are not.

> ONE-THIRD OF BUSINESS SCHOOL GRADUATES ARE WOMEN, YET ONLY 3 PERCENT OF TOP EXECUTIVES AT FORTUNE 500 COMPANIES ARE FEMALE.

I hope the times are a-changin', but as long as I'm still hearing the bit about women being "overly emotional," I'm going to go ahead and assume the myth is still prevalent, which might explain why more than one-third of business school graduates are women, yet only 3 percent of top executives at Fortune 500 companies are female.

Men are emotional, but their emotions present themselves as outbursts of temper—slamming fists on the table during meetings—and other physically obnoxious workplace behavior considered perfectly acceptable as long as the person raising his voice is a he. Women, on the other hand, tend to be less physically demonstrative, and their emotional outbursts usually consist of tears or near tears. I think both genders should rein it in a bit, but since we're just talking about the ladies here, why not find your poker face? We women are as strong as strong can be. We give birth (I'm hesitant to use this as an example since I haven't actually done it myself, but I hear that it's pretty darn difficult). We raise children (ditto). We cook and clean and work and manage households and do everything men can do, but backwards and in high heels, so to speak.

In her book *Fire with Fire,* Naomi Wolf advises women to drop the victim-loser image and stop playing second fiddle. "To imagine and enjoy winning . . . had long been alien to female consciousness," she writes. Because "history moves in response to narratives, dream images, heroes, heroines, and myths," women need to think of themselves as latter-day incarnations of "Diana, avenger of insult; Sheba, a responsible, politically influential sovereign; and Nike, the feminine spirit of victory." Channel your inner-avenger, goddess, warrior, or Betty Friedan. Prepare to have a lot of skinned knees and to not cry about it.

Emotions are not bad. No one wants to work for someone who seems like they're made of ice. You just have to learn how much, when, and where. Like many women, I tend to get very personally tied up in my work. On some level the company and I become one. Nothing can ruin my day like getting called to task about some mistake or another. In some businesses you have to let this go. Criticism builds character (I know, I don't like to hear that either). In one of my former jobs, I spent a lot of time receiving and responding to criticism. It was difficult to separate the job I was doing from the Me that I am. I needed a visual, so I printed a dozen little wallet-size cards that said "It's just a job" and put them in places where I knew I'd see them often. No one else knew what they meant, but the little card on my bulletin board that said "It's just a job" meant that *it* was a job—the job wasn't *me*. It helped me separate my work from my personal feelings about my work, which led to me being able to take criticism as if it was being directed at a separate entity other than myself. This helped end my having to sit in my car at lunchtime with the windows rolled up and the radio on to have a good cry. I even kept one of the cards on the dashboard of my car so it would remind me to let it go on my way home.

We are hard on ourselves, but in order to grow in our careers, we have to separate the personal from the professional. When someone criticizes your work, see it as a gift and a challenge. First, they're taking the time to offer criticism, so you must be worth it. Think about how often you've worked with people who seemed useless, unmotivated, and uninterested. Did you offer criticism? Probably not—and I doubt anyone else did either. People offer criticism because it matters whether or not you do a good job and, if they didn't think you could do it, why would they waste their time? The second positive thing about criticism is that it helps you discover that you can do better. Who wants to be in a job where you do the same thing over and over and it's perfect and nothing ever changes? Criticism is simply an analysis of your work. Put yourself in your boss's shoes (or the person who is in charge and offering criticism . . . it could be a client or a project-leading coworker), and you can see how difficult it is to offer a critique or advice on how to improve. In various management positions I've had to offer criticism to employees on everything from writing ability to interpersonal skills to body odor (yes, that was the worst one ever). It's not easy from either side of the desk.

THE EASIER YOU MAKE IT FOR YOUR BOSS TO GIVE YOU ADVICE, THE FASTER AND FARTHER YOU'RE GOING TO GO.

The good news is that, as women, we also have an uncanny ability to empathize. Try having some compassion for your boss (or supervisor or manager) the next time you're offered criticism on your work. You might even surprise her by thanking her for the criticism and telling her that you know it's difficult to offer feedback and that you appreciate her generosity. The easier you make it for your boss to give you advice, the faster and farther you're going to go.

LEARN WHOM YOU CAN AND CANNOT TRUST.

One of our more "feminine" traits is loyalty. Women tend to rate their job satisfaction much higher when we work with people we enjoy being around, when we develop friendships with coworkers, and when we respect our supervisors. You may have worked for your company for a long time, developed deep and lasting friendships, and grown closer to your work mates than you are to some family members. However, our natural inclination to use our feelings to gauge who we can trust at work can set us up for failure. The short answer: Trust no one. When it comes to your paycheck, you're the only one you should be relying on to advance your success. Sometimes putting trust in a coworker can actually put that coworker in the position of choosing between loyalty to you and her own job security. Which do you think she's going to choose?

TRUST NO ONE

Allison* has worked for the same boss at the same company for over six years. She puts in more late nights than early ones, has been commended time and time again for her performance, and never had a negative interim report.

*Names have been changed.

A few weeks before, Allison had brought a list of questions to one of the human resources staff, someone whom she trusted. She selected this person based on the nature of the information she would need to disclose in order to get her questions asked. Allison describes this woman, who we'll call Julie*, as "dear and caring, a great listener, very trustworthy." She asked Julie questions relating to what happens to her 401K contribution when she leaves the company, if she is 100 percent vested, and when would be a good time to put in notice. Allison was in the process of investigating the cost and benefits for the possibility of taking some time off for grad school. She had always been interested in pursuing a higher degree, despite the accomplishments she was making in the corporate world. She planned to stay in the field, but she wanted to build her education so she could command a higher salary down the road.

A third factor enters the equation: Allison's boss. It is no secret in the company that Allison's boss is difficult to get along with. Allison has even been commended by other higher-ups on her flexibility, easygoing nature, and ability to get along with difficult people. Julie answered her questions about the investment plan and asked several about what her intentions were. Allison felt comfortable enough to share: Part of the reason she had been looking into grad school is because she didn't know how much longer she could work for her boss. Julie said, "Not a surprise," and made sympathetic noises.

Two days later Julie had a meeting with her own boss, the HR manager, who happened to be close friends with Allison's boss. Allison was terminated the next day; reason given: attitude not conducive to building a team. Because Allison did not have a contract, the company was not a government agency, and the state that she lives in is an "at will" state, she had no legal recourse to retain her job or file for damages.

Is Julie a bitch for selling Allison out? Possibly. She may have also been intimidated into sharing confidential information by her HR manager. Had the information been made public, and Julie's boss discovered that she did

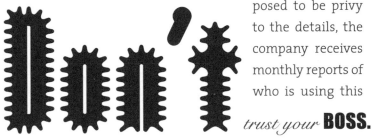

Don't *always trust your instincts on the job.*

not disclose what she knew, she could have been in trouble herself. Is Allison weak? She just trusted her own instincts. Based on this example, and many others like it, the advice is the same: Don't always trust your instincts on the job. Definitely don't trust anyone on the job. Don't trust your boss, don't trust the EAP (though legally your employer is not supposed to be privy to the details, the company receives monthly reports of who is using this *trust your* **BOSS.**

program and can generally get more information as needed from the program coordinator), and don't trust the benefits assistant. Call the insurance company yourself.

Even if you work with your very best friend, resist the urge to confide in your coworkers, especially if it involves intentions to leave the company. If you feel the need to complain about work, get some friends who don't work at the same company and hold weekly bitch sessions. As long as they have a job, they'll have some to share too.

By playing up your positive female traits—compassion, intuition, empathy, loyalty—you can learn how to handle the negatives and never again give anyone the ammunition to say that women are too emotional to run companies.

Never:
Bake for the office.

Why Not?
It doesn't matter if you're a prize-winning pastry chef—you're not the den mother. If you bring baked or otherwise homemade goods to the office, you will reflexively be relegated to the role of "office mom." And the office mom doesn't get promoted to vice president. She gets to clean up the lunchroom and bring cookies.

But I'm a great cook, you think? Super. Bring your culinary masterpieces to your book club, your monthly meeting at your local women's center, or to the nearest firehouse (they love it). Just don't bring it to the office. Resist the urge to show off your cooking skills and focus instead on your work-related talents.

What about potluck work functions? Didn't I already say no baking for coworkers? If you're worried about being rude by not bringing a covered dish (and why any office is still having potluck instead of a catered lunch by outside professionals is a whole other chapter), do bring something. But pick it up at a deli, or offer to bring two-liter sodas, chips, cups, paper plates, or anything else that doesn't require baking skills. I simply say, "I don't cook. What shall I bring?" I'm not lying when I say I don't cook—I can cook and I actually like to cook, I just choose not to when it comes to work functions. But I cook all the time for my friends and family. And I did bring my famous Mediterranean couscous apricot chicken salad to the office once, because I live alone and the recipe makes lots, but I made every single person in the office that day promise and swear that they'd never see me as the mom (most said I had nothing to worry about, though they enjoyed the food).

P.S. This rule applies to men as well. The office is no place for domesticity, whether you are male or female.

Never:

Cry in the office.

Why Not?

One: It's unseemly. **Two:** It's poor form. **Three:** The only thing it accomplishes is a black mark on your reputation that may never go away (see Chapter 6: Damage Control: You Break It, You Fix It).

If you're unable to control your urge to burst into tears, it's better to leave the area with a flimsy excuse than to stay and cry. Keep Visine and an eye makeup repair kit in your car, cry it out with the windows rolled up and radio on, patch yourself up, and get back to work.

If you're having personal problems that may lead to an inability to control your tears—a death in the family, a breakup with your boyfriend, financial woes—it's better to take a sick day than to come into the office and try and control it. I'm not telling you not to cry. I cry all the time. I just take it outside or keep it at home.

Never:
Stab coworkers in the back.

Why Not?

Women have a reputation of not playing well with our own gender. I've heard, time and time again, stories from women who say they would prefer to work in an office full of men to working in one full of women, where they feel they have to watch their backs. I've heard that women are more vicious than men, that they'll cut you off at the knees and stab you in the back to get ahead. I disagree. I think both men and women behave unethically in work situations; it's just more shocking when women do it.

There's also the issue of the old boy's club. Men support each other, even if they feel threatened, because they understand that there's enough to go around for all of us. Women should do the same. I've used every opportunity in my career to give another woman a hand up, whether a coworker or someone I'm mentoring. Women do tend to appear cattier than men, but that's only because society places us in that role.

Malicious gossip and manipulation bring our entire gender down a notch. Women's networking groups tend not to work as well as men's because we haven't seemed to learn to play well with others. We're jealous of each other's success, rather than complimentary. We'll spread rumors about a coworker who scored the corner office and speculate on how she got there. This kind of behavior is a black mark on our gender and must be stopped. You don't have to change every woman—just start with you. If a coworker begins to speculate on a female boss's promotion, stop her. We must band together if we're ever going to make the Fortune 500 list look like an accurate representation of gender in business.

Never:
Blame bad behavior on hormones or PMS.

Why Not?
There's enough of that coming from the men in corporate America. Men love to say that women become

bitches at "that time of the month." We don't have to fall in line. You and I both know that PMS sucks, but it doesn't impact our lives to the extent that we can blame mistakes at work on our hormone levels. We don't have to pretend we're genderless, or that we don't have vaginas, for that matter.

Think about how you would react if a male coworker blamed a temper tantrum or outburst on his excess testosterone levels?

You screwed up, maybe you lost your temper, you're not concentrating today—whatever the reason, your apology to whomever should not include the words "PMS," "time of the month," or "hormonal." Making statements like these only means you won't be taken seriously when it's important for you to be taken seriously. Not to mention that you're contributing to the entire mythology that makes "acting like a girl" a derogatory statement.

Tell the truth: You were having a bad day, you made a mistake, you made an error in judgment, you were wrong. It's not so difficult.

Along the same lines, never cite "female problems" or "cramps" as reasons for calling in sick or leaving the office early. It's always best (unless you have a highly infectious illness and have been required by the health department to inform anyone you've been in contact with) to simply say, "I'm not well," and leave it at that. Think about it: Would you really want the gory specifics if one of your employees called in sick? I prefer "I'm sick" over a way-too-detailed explanation about a sinus infection or anything that includes the word discharge. Besides, if your cramps are so bad that you can't show up to work, you have problems more serious than whether or not you're calling in sick.

Never:
Gossip.

Why Not?

At least stop the gossiping about coworkers. It doesn't make you look good to discuss someone else's shortcomings, and chances are they're talking about yours, too. In order to change negative stereotypes that are inherent in our culture—such as the image of women as gossiping fishwives— you have to start with yourself. No company head in his or her right mind is going to promote someone who appears to enjoy malicious rumors, whether you're spreading them or just being an active listener. Even if you're not the one gossiping, you're participating by hearing it. How do you stop other people from bringing you down with them? I've found that being honest works quite well. A simple "I'd rather not discuss this behind someone's back" is sufficient. Or, "I'm not comfortable talking about Ann when she's not here to defend herself."

When men talk about coworkers in the same way, no one calls it gossip. It's called conversation. It sucks, but the stereotypes are there, and we have to make ourselves impervious to criticism.

No matter how much you love it, gossip is not your friend. It might be entertaining, but it can kill your career. If you must gossip, do so with friends outside of work.

CHAPTER FIVE

MYTHS AND FAIRY TALES

These days it is still difficult to find many examples of female CEOs and business leaders after which to model your own career. I can come up with a few:

Carly Fiorina, *former President and CEO of Hewlett-Packard;*

Cathy Hughes, *CEO of Radio One (and the first African-American woman to head a publicly traded firm in the United States);*

Andrea Jung, *CEO of Avon;*

Shelley Lazarus, *Chairman and CEO of Ogilvy & Mather Worldwide;*

Anne Mulcahy, *Chairman and CEO of Xerox Corp.;*

and Anita Roddick, *founder and CEO of The Body Shop.*

Carly and Anita both wrote books (good ones).

But I grew up a child of the 1980s, and these women had yet to make their mark. And because I lived in a somewhat isolated world of military bases and military towns, I had little exposure to women in leadership roles. I was a young adult before I realized that I really didn't have to look very far for a role model.

Although as a little girl I kept hearing over and over that I could be anything I wanted to be, I was confused by the mixed message of having a mother who was at home cleaning and doing laundry and a father who was gone exploring the world for months at a time. I knew that things weren't that simple. My mother also attended consciousness-raising groups, read *Ms. Magazine,* and occasionally took college classes when child care was available. But when my mother wasn't around, it was my older sisters who were primary caregivers, not my father.

ALTHOUGH AS A LITTLE GIRL
I KEPT HEARING OVER AND OVER
THAT I COULD BE ANYTHING I WANTED TO BE,
I WAS CONFUSED BY THE MIXED MESSAGE
OF HAVING A **MOTHER** WHO WAS
AT HOME CLEANING AND DOING LAUNDRY...

At eleven years old I was old enough to have heard the derogatory comments my father made about my mother's career ambitions and to have witnessed the expensive gifts of household appliances that made my mother rage about how easy it would have been for my father to write a check for her continuing education instead of a new dishwasher, Radar Range, or living room furniture. And when my mother managed to pay for tuition anyway with a part-time job and student loans, I heard the arguments about what a woman's role at home should be and the derisiveness of those statements through her bedroom walls. Meanwhile, the *Electric Company* and *Free to Be You and Me* sang songs through the Curtis Mathes floor model television about every girl growing to be her own woman and how I could be anything I set my mind to.

When my father told us he was moving out, I thought, *Good, now we can be a real family.* By real family, I meant a happy mother and happy children. Going to college and working made my mother happy and that made me happy.

Once it was just the girls in the house, my mother finished college and went back for a second degree. She worked two jobs—one in the daytime and one on the nights she didn't have class. I learned what "no alimony" meant and thought it was exciting to live in an apartment instead of a house, in the city instead of way out in the country. I thought my mother was like Ann Romano, the mom on *One Day at a Time* (a 1980s sitcom about a divorced woman who moves to Indianapolis with her daughters to start a new life for themselves). Even when my mother had to start selling cosmetics so she could afford to pay for her school books, we were still happy. We helped our mother pack the little pink cases and tubes of face cream before she went to sales parties. We quizzed her from textbooks with titles like *Measures in Clinical Practice* and *Paradigms of Clinical Social Work*. When I was in high school, I attended my mother's graduation ceremony and cried when she walked across the stage in her robes to accept her master's degree.

... AND A **FATHER** WHO WAS GONE EXPLORING THE WORLD FOR MONTHS AT A TIME.

And we all lived happily ever after.

"*What you* RISK *reveals What you* VALUE"

~ JEANETTE WINTERSON, WRITER

There are all kinds of fairy tales. Mine isn't the same as yours, but given the number of single-parent households headed by a female parent, it very well might be. My mother took a lot of flack for her decision. She was a military wife during a time when being an officer's wife should have been enough. It wasn't. Should she have fought her desire to have a career of her own and stayed home, I think I would not be the person I am—nor would my three sisters. We all have a strong work ethic. I am a part of Generation X. By all rights, I should be a full-on slacker (or at least should have spent the better part of my twenties that way), and achievement should be low on my list of priorities. All three of my sisters have children and all three have careers. And though my mother was on solid financial standing by the time I was in high school, she willingly signed an emancipated minor statement so that I could get a part-time job when I was fifteen because I wanted to make my own money. Making your own money is something my mother believes in.

It would be too easy for me to be angry at my father for being the man he was. I think the fact that my mother is the woman that she is, and that we all became the women we are, cancels out the negative. What I *am* angry about, some twenty-odd years later, is that there are still people who think a woman's primary role is to stay home and care for her children and, as a result, if that woman does get a job it's for "extra" money or "household expenses."

FACT: THE MAJORITY OF WOMEN WORK BECAUSE OF ECONOMIC NEED. IN MAY 1986 TWO-THIRDS OF WORKING MOTHERS WITH CHILDREN AT HOME SAID THEY WORKED TO SUPPORT THEIR FAMILY (THAT NUMBER INCLUDED MY MOTHER AND HER THREE JOBS). IN 1992, 44 PERCENT OF WOMEN IN THE LABOR FORCE WERE EITHER SINGLE (24 PERCENT), DIVORCED (12 PERCENT), WIDOWED (4 PERCENT), OR SEPARATED (4 PERCENT). WOMEN'S NEED FOR GOOD JOBS IS DEMONSTRATED BY THE FACT THAT NEARLY 45 PERCENT OF ALL FAMILY HOUSEHOLDS MAINTAINED BY WOMEN LIVED IN POVERTY IN 2000.

~Source: Wider Opportunities for Women, www.work4women.org

THE LEGEND OF THE WAGE GAP

It seems astounding that there is still so much misinformation out there about women's position in the job market. Some dispute the fact that women age sixteen and older working full-time earned on average 80.4 percent of men's median earnings (Bureau of Labor Statistics, 2004). I've heard many "justifications" for these figures, mostly from men, but sometimes from women, saying that the statistics are skewed because: (1) women stay home with children, (2) women are undereducated, and (3) men work longer hours than women (those are the top three—the others are more ridiculous and vary from suggesting that men start working when they are younger to stating that women are unable to perform in "high-paying jobs requiring physical labor" (and I thought those were the lower paying jobs).

In 2006, during a May 12 appearance on ABC's *Good Morning America,* John Stossel, cohost of ABC's *20/20,* disputed the facts and figures about the wage gap, claiming that it is a "myth" that "women earn less" than men for "doing the same work." He was on the show promoting his latest book and argued that if the statistics were true, "all the employers that hired men would go out of business, because they'd be paying their workforce too much." Faulty logic aside, Stossel did agree there was a wage gap, but he attributed it to the fact that "men are more willing to take lousy jobs, work longer, be away from our families. Women make good choices for their families and happiness, they live the best life, and that's why they earn less." As if I needed another reason to dislike John Stossel.

The Bureau of Labor Statistics, an unbiased government agency, compiled wage data in 2004 for full-time wage and salary workers age sixteen and older. According to the data women earned on average 80.4 percent of men's weekly median earnings. In fact in every occupation for which the organization gathered data, men earned a higher median wage than women, regardless of job title.

Additionally, undercutting the theory that men earn more than women because they simply work longer hours, the nonpartisan Economic Policy Institute's analysis of average hourly wages by gender found that, in addition to earning higher salaries, men earned more than women on an hourly basis. In 2003 most men earned between $7.46 and $43.48 an hour, compared with $6.67 to $33.40 for women's hourly earnings.

GAP

Still think the gender wage gap is a myth? Full reports from the Economic Policy Institute, including men's and women's real hourly wages by education and labor force participation rates by occupation, are available to the public at *www.epinet.org*. The Bureau of Labor Statistics' Web site has up-to-date wage data by occupation and gender compiled for more than two hundred occupations at *www.bls.gov.*

In addition, the National Association for Female Executives (NAFE), using data compiled "from surveys by private organizations, federal agencies, and consulting companies," detailed the wage gap between men and women professionals in select industries in its 2005 Annual Salary Survey. NAFE found that women consistently earned less than men. For instance, as illustrated below, women in the accounting industry earned less than their male counterparts, regardless of work experience.

Average total compensation, including salary and bonus

JOB EXPERIENCE	WOMEN	MEN
1-5 years	$66,957	$115,024
6-10 years	$70,512	$93,896
11-15 years	$80,986	$99,631
16-20 years	$100, 879	$114,037
More than 20 years	$95,544	$118,282

Source: National Association for Female Executives (NAFE)

How much of the wage gap can be attributed to discrimination is difficult to figure, and is controversial, but estimates from the Institute for Women's Policy Research *(www .iwpr.org)* say it's between one-quarter and one-third. How much really should be irrelevant at this point, since we've already spent too much time pointing fingers. We need to move away from blame and toward a solution.

Arm yourself with facts and logic, then start fighting for your fair share.

MYTH VS. FACT

Myth: Men make better CEOs.

FACT: Men make *more* CEOs, but that's only because people believe fables like "men are more aggressive" or "men are cutthroat." It's irresponsible to make broad, sweeping statements like this about either gender. I've known women who are more cutthroat in the business world than any man you'll ever meet. I've seen women walk into boardrooms à la Joan Crawford addressing PepsiCo ("don't f*ck with me fellas, this ain't my first time at the rodeo"), bring an out-of-control meeting to attention, close on a merger agreement, and book a flight to another city to meet with employees for a company we just bought—all in the space of ten minutes.

Women are natural nurturers and problem solvers, no matter how assertive, aggressive, and ambitious we are. Every company in the world is about the bottom line; without it, our economy would crash and anarchy would ensue. Companies are getting smarter and beginning to realize that gender diversity is beneficial to their bottom line. Where men fail, women can succeed—and vice versa. Gone are the days of choosing the "right man for the job." Logically, considering that companies are placing higher value on the cost savings of employee retention and having a compassionate business model, corporate America is waking up to the fact that oftentimes the right man for the job is a woman. We're not asking to replace every male CEO with a female. What we do want is an accurate representation of the gender balance in corporate America on the list of CEOs in corporate America.

Myth: Women are too emotional to be in charge.
FACT: I've been calling bullshit on this one since 1992. I simply cannot be both the "bitch in the room" *and* the "cry baby." It is true that we've grown up in a society where it is OK for girls

I SIMPLY CANNOT BE BOTH THE
BITCH IN THE ROOM *and the* CRY BABY.

to show emotion and not OK for boys to do the same. But the women I've encountered in business know how to channel their emotions and use them for good and not evil. It's the same argument we get about having a female president, as if a crying jag and a hormonal surge could result in Ms. President pushing the button or starting a war for no good reason.

Being emotional is not a bad thing. I've yet to work with a female in a management position who fell apart on the job, and I've worked with women under an extraordinary amount of stress—in rapidly growing companies, in companies getting ready for an initial public offering (stock makes everyone crazy), and in the midst of personal situations that would make me want to crawl back into bed in the morning instead of doing battle in corporate America.

IT IS TRUE THAT WE'VE GROWN UP IN A SOCIETY WHERE IT IS OK FOR GIRLS TO SHOW EMOTION AND NOT OK FOR BOYS TO DO THE SAME.

As far as women not being good bosses, the fastest-growing segment of new small businesses is comprised of female owners—women who create their own workplaces don't have to fight discrimination in someone else's.

Myth: The wage gap isn't real.
FACT: The wage gap is real. There are several studies by non-partisan and unbiased (and governmental) agencies—including the Economic Policy Institute and the Bureau of Labor Statistics—that support the very real gap between what women earn in comparison to their male counterparts. We don't know how much of the gap can be attributed to gender discrimination, but the fact that the wage gap exists is indisputable. The bottom line is that there is no valid reason for women to earn less than their male counterparts.

Myth: Certain jobs are "men's work" and other jobs are "women's work."
FACT: Attitudes about which jobs are appropriate for men and which ones are appropriate for women are the result of

tradition and socialization. The vast majority of job requirements are unrelated to gender. The only jobs I can think of that are gender specific would be those requiring a penis (for men) or breasts and/or vagina (for women). Besides waiting tables at Hooter's, I believe the rest would fall under "sex work," and we're not here to talk about that.

THERE ARE MORE SINGLE-PARENT FEMALE HEADS OF HOUSEHOLDS IN THE UNITED STATES THAN EVER BEFORE, MAKING THE ARGUMENT THAT MEN ARE BREADWINNERS NULL AND VOID.

Myth: Women always leave the workplace to get married or have babies.

FACT: In March 1992, on average, women were found to work thirty years over the course of their lifetimes, regardless of whether or not they married. Of those women who do leave the workplace to have children, more than half return when the child is one year old or younger. By the time the youngest child is three years old, at least six out of every ten mothers have entered or returned to the labor force.

Source: www.work4women.org

Myth: Men should make more money, because they are the "breadwinners" for the family.

FACT: Although more women than men are the main caregiver in their families, more and more fathers are staying home and taking care of their children while the mother works, more fathers are participating equally in the housework and child care in their family, and more fathers have sole or shared custody of their children in situations of divorce. Additionally there are more single-parent female heads of households in the United States than ever before, making the argument that men are breadwinners null and void.

Myth: A woman's place is in the home.
FACT: In 1994, women accounted for 46 percent of the total labor force. Nearly two-thirds of all women age sixteen and over were in the labor force in 1991. Women accounted for 62 percent of total labor force growth between 1980 and 1991, and two out of every three workers entering the labor force between 1990 and 2005 were women. The majority of women work because of economic necessity, and nontraditional jobs better enable women to support themselves and their families.
Source: www.work4women.org

Myth: Gender bias has largely been eradicated. If women don't succeed in the workplace, it's because they don't want to.
FACT: While women make up one-third of business school graduates, they remain stuck in middle management. According to 2005 data from *Fortune* magazine's Fortune 500 list, average growth in the percentage of corporate officer positions held by women fell dramatically to 0.23 percentage points per year, the lowest yearly gain in the past ten years. Between 2002 and 2005, the total number of women corporate officers increased by a mere 0.7 percentage points to 16.4 percent.
Source: www.feminist.org

GENDER BIAS

Myth: Married women who have husbands to support them should stay home and leave the good paying jobs for men.
FACT: Many American families are unable to support themselves on a single income. Additionally, according to the U.S. Department of Labor, even if all the employed married women

gave their jobs to unemployed men, there would still be 1.2 million unfilled jobs.

Myth: Women leave the workforce to have babies, costing companies big bucks.
FACT: More than half of women who leave a job to have a baby return within a year; 60 percent do so within three years. Health problems more commonly associated with men, including alcohol abuse and stress-related illnesses, are likely far more costly to corporate America than maternity leave.
Source: www.work4women.org

Myth: Women's brains are genetically programmed to make them less suitable for careers in science and engineering.
FACT: In fact, science makes use of traditional "female" skills like communication, creativity, and ability to work in groups. Cultural stereotypes reinforced at all levels of schooling and the way science careers are structured do more to keep women underrepresented than their DNA.
Source: www.mentornet.net

FIGHTING STEREOTYPES

Many myths about women and work come from stereotypes of women's behavior on the job. Persistent, ambitious, and assertive women are "bitches." Women with strong opinions are "pushy." Confident women are "arrogant." Even when we behave just like men, we're slotted into these unpleasant descriptive categories based on gender. And gender stereotypes can block advancement.

Men aren't the only ones perpetuating stereotypes. A 2005 report, *Women "Take Care," Men "Take Charge,"* by Catalyst, a U.S. research and advisory organization dedicated to advancing women at work, says that the effects of gender-based stereotyping can be devastating, potentially undermining women's capacity to lead and posing serious challenges to women's career advancement. In the study both men and women respondents cast women as better at stereotypically feminine "caretaking skills" such as supporting and rewarding.

 aren't the only ones perpetuating stereotypes.

Both men and women asserted that men excel at more conventionally masculine "taking charge" skills such as influencing superiors and delegating responsibility. Compounding this, it also appears that exposure to women leaders does not necessarily lessen stereotyping. Indeed it often reinforces it, creating "extreme perceptions" of women leaders. But despite the fact that companies have shown an increased commitment to diversity, inclusion, and the advancement of women in the workplace, the representation of women in leadership remains stagnant. The study also argues that unless companies take steps to eradicate this bias, women leaders will always be undermined and misjudged, regardless of their talents or aptitudes.

Even if your company isn't making this kind of effort, you can make some modifications to your own behavior that obliges others to react in a more positive way.

GO GET 'EM

In most jobs, we're expected to be self-confident. And particularly in sales positions, we're trained to be assertive. Good salespeople are described as "bulldogs"—they latch on and won't let go. Men are applauded for this behavior, while many women are treated like yappy Chihuahuas for the same characteristics.

Typically the word *aggressive* is used to describe behavior that's pushy, abrasive, or forceful. In contrast, the dictionary defines *assertive* as "persistently positive or confident." The real difference between being assertive and being aggressive is how our words and behavior affect other people. Assertive communication supports our own rights while still taking the feelings of others into consideration. In short, assertive behavior shows respect and aggressive behavior does not.

One of the most insidious reactions women have had as a result of negative stereotypes is to pull back, often running in the other direction. I've encountered too many soft-spoken, demure women who wonder why they're not making sales or getting promoted. I can tell from their body language and use of the passive voice that they're probably being passed over because they've become as charismatic as dishrags. And even though I know the answer, I always ask them when was the last time they asked for a raise or promotion (or sale or new account). The response is usually some form of "why bother?" They feel trapped in a catch-22, damned if they do and damned if they don't. "I was told to tone it down," one friend told me. "So I did."

HOW TO BE ASSERTIVE

HOW TO BE ASSERTIVE
WITHOUT TRIPPING THE BITCH ALARM

Use active voice in all communication. (That includes e-mail.) "I plan to close five new contracts this month" makes a stronger statement than, "Maybe I'll make some cold calls." Active voice is specific.

Be your own champion. Don't be afraid that making your boss aware of your accomplishments will be seen as bragging. You should be proud of your work, and sending an "FYI" e-mail to your boss about the new accounts you scored this month shows that you care about your success.

Read other people's body language and react appropriately. This means you'll have to pay attention to nonverbal cues like eye contact (or lack thereof) and respond accordingly. If you're rambling on and on to a coworker about how great your last sale was and she's not hanging on your every word, wrap it up.

Make sure your body language matches your message. If you tell a coworker (or your boss) how pleased you are about the company's latest acquisition, but appear sullen or less than energetic, you won't come across as sincere. No one likes a faker.

Learn how to take a compliment. Don't disparage yourself when someone praises you or offers a kind word. A simple "thank you" is much better than, "Yeah, I was surprised I managed to swing that." Belittling yourself only makes other people feel uncomfortable, and you'll betray your own self-doubt.

Temper your disagreement. If you don't know how someone else feels about a topic, you can still make your opinion heard in a straightforward and nonjudgmental way. If that doesn't get the message across, you can make a stronger point by asking questions that make it clear that you disagree. Instead of saying "I thought you meant," ask, "What did you mean?" It's always better to give someone else the opportunity to explain before you prove them wrong.

Speak up for yourself. If you have to say no, do it without over-apologizing. Offer a brief explanation and let it go. Otherwise you become the office chump, and everyone will dump his or her work on you without a second thought.

Be confident. Don't feel pressured to justify or explain every decision you make. Sometimes it's best to make the decision, follow through, and deal with the consequences later. We learn our best lessons by allowing ourselves to make mistakes (and often, our first instincts are spot-on).

Don't be a victim. Assertive people are problem solvers, not victims of circumstances beyond their control. There is always (always!) something we can do to reach a solution.

Don't be passive-aggressive. Conflict at work is best met head-on. Instead of wasting time by gossiping and complaining, focus on the positive, productive steps you can take to solve problems.

Stop apologizing. It's infuriating, but many women do this reflexively, even when entirely unnecessary. Eliminate the phrase "I'm sorry, but" from your vocabulary. Save your apologies for when you really screw up.

THE BOTTOM LINE: IF YOU DON'T STAND UP FOR YOURSELF, NO ONE WILL. NOTHING HAPPENS WITHOUT ACTION, AND ACTION CANNOT OCCUR WITHOUT ASSERTIVE BEHAVIOR. ONCE YOU'VE DISARMED THE NAYSAYERS, YOU CAN STOP PROCRASTINATING QUIETLY BEHIND YOUR DESK AND START MOVING FORWARD.

DAMAGE CONTROL: YOU BREAK IT, YOU FIX IT

Well, you've gotten this far. You're ready to set your inner-CEO (or inner-Betty) free. There's just one problem: *You've been breaking all the rules.*

You bake your famous Magic Cookie Bars and bring them to the office at least once a month. You've cried in front of your boss or your coworkers. Your boss has been denying your requests for a salary increase for years, citing the fact that you have a husband as reason to keep you at your entry-level salary, despite the fact that you're basically doing his job.

So what do you do now? Quit? Find another job where no one knows you so you can start over?

That might not be necessary. As long as there's no written record in your employment file about your frequent crying jags, and you haven't signed a contract stating that you are the official Magic Cookie Bar bringer for all-time, you can still recover. *You can start over right where you are, starting ... now.*

First, stop it. Stop the baking, stop the crying, stop the gossiping, and stop *asking* for raises. **It's never too late to start over** (unless you're dating your married boss, or unmarried boss for that matter ... in that case, I'd recommend freshening up your résumé and start looking for a new place to apply your new rules).

I lead workshops for young women about gender issues at work, including my no baking rule. In many of the sessions, the reaction to some of my rules have been mixed: "But I like to bake," one woman said. "Great," I responded. "But don't bake for work." Because the workshops were about women's issues at work, the groups were almost strictly all female—except for one.

During that workshop I noticed one lone older gentleman in the audience and did my best to make him feel welcome. I knew who he was, being that the workshop was in my hometown and it's not New York City. He was the regional head of a large southern banking institution, someone I would have put into the "Good Old Boys" category, because that's how my brain works. After the workshop he came up and introduced himself, said he enjoyed the session, and I thought that was that. A few weeks later the woman who organized the conference called to tell me she heard from Mr. Bank Executive. "Really?" I asked, thinking that she was going to tell me he thought I was brash or uppity, two categories I thought "Good Old Boys" liked to put women with opinions in. But I was wrong. He'd gotten in touch to tell her that, on the Monday following the conference, he called a meeting of all local corporate staff and informed them that the women in the office would no longer be providing food for meetings. In fact he said no one would be bringing food into the office unless it was from a catering company. He told the conference organizer that it hadn't occurred to him previously that many of these women felt compelled to provide food for meetings and company events, and that by doing so they might be impacting their ca-

> PERHAPS BOTH SEXES SIMPLY NEED TO BE ENLIGHTENED ABOUT HOW OUR SUBCONSCIOUS MINDS RESPOND TO MALE AND FEMALE ROLES.

reers with his company. He respects women and wants them to have the same advantage as his male employees.

It wasn't the first time my stereotype radar had been wrong, but it was so far off that it made me rethink my whole judgmental attitude about male CEOs. It made me wonder how many times in the past I'd been guilty of assuming a malevolent conspiracy against women in the workplace, when the truth is that women were the ones who set up the standards in the first place. Perhaps both sexes simply need to be enlightened about how our subconscious minds respond to male and female roles.

Lesson learned. I no longer view the typical white male CEO as the enemy. In fact many of them (including several I now work with) have a great deal of respect for women in the workplace. From time to time I still run across a few who have their female secretaries handle their personal business (like shopping for the wife's birthday present) or require the only female sales rep in the office to double as the receptionist or

In order to promote equity in the workplace,
we have to be able to live up to the same expectations as our male counterparts,
which include not having
breakdowns *and* **temper tantrums** *in the office.*

expect women who work in the same building as the company president to always wear panty hose, but I'm starting to believe that these men are the exception and not the rule.

In order to promote equity in the workplace, we have to be able to live up to the same expectations as our male counterparts, which include not having breakdowns and temper tantrums in the office. Men tend to handle damage control differently—they suck it up (because they've been doing that since Little League), apologize, shake it off, and move on. They recognize that it isn't personal.

You don't have to be emotionless at work—passion, after all, makes the world go 'round—but you do have to be able to control your emotions. A passionate statement when speaking to your boss about the obstacles you're dealing with at work has a stronger impact when you're not in tears. If you have crossed that line, and most of us have, the best way to handle the situation is to excuse and compose yourself and return to your boss's office to continue the conversation *after* leading with a frank apology. Don't make excuses; a simple "I'm sorry I momentarily lost control of my emotions and it won't happen again" will suffice. If your outburst completely freaked your boss out (and you'll be able to tell), it's OK to add, "I am really passionate about this, and I just let it get out of hand temporarily. I'm fine now, and I'm ready to continue our conversation."

THE OTHER KIND OF MISTAKES

Unless you're Ms. Perfect (and we both know you're not), you're eventually going to screw up a big project, blow a deadline, or make the wrong decision. Because men usually learn to deal with competition at an early age, between team sports and society's expectations that they keep their emotions in check, they are also usually more capable of separating their feelings from their work. Women, on the other hand, tend to see setbacks and mistakes at work as personal failures and reflections on their overall abilities. To be better at damage control, we can take a few lessons from our male counterparts.

So your worst nightmare (or second worst, right after the one about showing up for a test naked) came true and you made a major mistake on the job. The project you were in charge of tanked. You lost a major client because of a miscommunication. You made a judgment call that was way off base, and now you have to deal with the consequences. I'm a firm believer that few things are beyond fixing, as long as you take responsibility. How you deal with it is what counts.

First, repeat after me: "It's just my job." Because it *is* just your job. It isn't who you are, it isn't the end of the world, it isn't going to kill you, and even if it does, it won't matter once you're gone anyway. No one ever says on their deathbed, "I wish I'd handled that deal better."

Second, don't try to smokescreen or redirect blame. Even if the mistake wasn't entirely your fault, a savvy manager or CEO will always take one for the team. Not doing so is a sign of weakness. Don't blame someone who works with you or for you. It's your project, you were in charge, it was your client (and definitely don't blame the client—let your boss do that), and you have to step up.

> **NO ONE WANTS TO HEAR A LITANY OF EXCUSES.** IN THE BUSINESS WORLD, MENDING FENCES AND FIXING WHAT'S BROKEN IS WAY MORE IMPORTANT THAN WHO IS AT FAULT.

Be honest. Bring it to your boss's attention as soon as possible and take responsibility for whatever decision you made that led to the mistake. Explain the circumstances without blaming anyone else, be frank about the reason you made the mistake, and find out what your boss needs you to do to run damage control. You might have to call a client and smooth things over, scrap a project and start over from scratch, or change workflow or policy to ensure it doesn't happen

96

again. The most important thing you can communicate to your boss is that a mistake has been made and you want to know what you can do to fix it. Let her know you want to help devise a strategy for preventing such a mistake from happening again.

Be in control. No matter how large the error, your boss will likely react positively to your confidence that (a) it won't happen again and (b) you're going to fix it. A good boss allows employees to take risks and make mistakes—and promotes those who know how to handle the big ones.

Follow through. Do exactly what you and your boss decided would be the best method to fix your mistake. Ignoring it is certainly easier, but it won't go away. Once you've devised the plan and executed it, schedule a follow up "postgame" meeting with your boss to give her the lowdown on how it went, what the next step will be, and any other pertinent information. Be positive, even if you have to fake it. Do this every time you make a mistake, and your boss will have endless confidence in your ability to handle sticky situations.

Don't be afraid to do it again. The only reason we make mistakes on the job is because we take risks. Some of them pan out, others don't. It's always going to be hit or miss, and you have to learn to handle the misses right along with celebrating the hits. Hopefully you'll have more of the latter, but don't let one mistake take the wind out of your sails (or sales). Confidence in your own abilities is key to being successful, and one mistake doesn't mean you're incompetent. I see it as a way to "test my powers"—working outside of my comfort zone to see just how far I can go and how much I can achieve.

Learn something. Every mistake is an opportunity to obtain experience. Most of the successful people I know have failed time and time again before achieving success. The difference between them and other people who fail is that they treat mistakes like educational opportunities—either they know what not to do next time, or they discover their own limits and compensate by improving their skills or technical expertise through training.

"It is not enough for you to do your very best. You must do what is REQUIRED *of the situation."*

~ CATHY HUGHES, CEO OF RADIO ONE AND
THE FIRST AFRICAN-AMERICAN WOMAN TO HEAD
A PUBLICLY TRADED FIRM IN THE UNITED STATES

REINVENTING YOUR REPUTATION

Some of the mistakes we make at work are not even remotely work related. We all know we shouldn't date our boss or coworkers, but it happens. We shouldn't send bitchy e-mails about coworkers, and definitely shouldn't accidentally send said bitchy e-mails to the coworker in question. We shouldn't get drunk at the holiday party and end the evening by kneeling before a potted plant to throw up an evening's worth of hors d'oeuvres and seven Cosmopolitans.

No matter what happened and whatever the reason, the deed is done. You really screwed up, and now you're the Office Tramp, Office Bitch, or Office Drunk.

I could tell a dozen stories about friends who've dated their bosses, made pretty severe e-mail faux pas, or danced on tables at a work function after being slightly overserved—but they'd probably hunt me down and exact some twisted revenge. What I can say is that I've made a few of these mistakes myself, witnessed many others, and have yet to find a case that couldn't be managed after the fact.

OFFICE TRAMP

Dating at work is a no-no. Many companies even have firm policies against it. Others have an implied and unspoken ethical contract. In any office with more than a few male and female employees, especially if those employees are in their twenties, it's going to happen. In fact I remember reading a statistic about how many married couples met at work that was ridiculously high. You can date at work if you're mature about it, selective, and open with your boss or HR department.

I once dated someone I worked with when I worked for a company that had a "no dating in the same department" policy. We kept it off everyone's radar for a long time (long enough to get past the "I like you" stage), then he applied for a transfer to another department right before I was promoted to manager. A good thing, because I would have been his boss. It didn't work out, but since he transferred to another department, I didn't have to see his face every day (or him, mine), and everyone was happy. Had we not maintained professional distance at work, I'm positive we both would have lost credibility. Even once it was out in the open, there were no PDAs (public displays of affection) at work or at work events.

EXTRICATING YOURSELF FROM A RELATIONSHIP WITH YOUR BOSS IS GOING TO BE TRICKY. Let's just say you've been dating men from the office, perhaps even your boss. (Do I even need to say that's the **biggest no-no** of all?) Your coworkers speak in hushed tones when you walk by their offices. You know you're the subject of gossip. The first thing you need to ask yourself is whether your career or your relationship(s) is more important. If the answer is your relationships, skip to Chapter 10: Moving On, and immediately begin looking for another job.

If the answer is your career, put an end to using the office as your personal dating service.

Extricating yourself from a relationship with your boss is going to be tricky. You're going to need to do three things: One, end it immediately and kindly. Two, be honest and explain that your career has to come first. And three, stay away. Don't call him outside of work, don't send him instant messages, and by all means, don't accidentally slip up one night when you've had a few cocktails at happy hour and feel lonely. Make sure he understands that it isn't him, *it's you.* You're sorry he's in the kind of marriage that makes him feel like he needs to look elsewhere (don't accuse; you're not in any position to judge, home wrecker), but things happen and you're concerned your reputation is at stake. If it's serious enough so that he plans on leaving his wife **(which almost never happens, by the way),** and you think you might be in love, then the two of you should discuss which one is going to leave the company. Regardless, sometimes it is better to start fresh somewhere else with a clean slate.

OFFICE BITCH

So you and your cubicle buddy have an ongoing joke about how many days another coworker goes between washing her hair, or you have a particularly hilarious nickname for your boss that you felt compelled to share via e-mail. Except instead of e-mailing your friend, you accidentally sent the e-mail to the subject of your bitchy remarks, to your boss, or (God forbid) every employee in the company. I've seen it happen multiple times. When I worked for a software company, it happened almost every time we got a slew of new hires who weren't accustomed to working on a company network. It's almost too easy to type a name in the **To** address field in your e-mail that defaults to the wrong person, or to hit **Reply All** when you meant to forward the e-mail. Every few weeks we'd get an all-employees e-mail with some smart-ass response to an employee-policy e-mail. Talk about starting off on the wrong foot. You don't want to be the new employee who mocked an e-mail from HR, trust me.

> **TIP:** DEPENDING ON HOW SOON YOU'RE AWARE THAT YOU MADE THE MISTAKE, IT IS POSSIBLE TO RECALL THE E-MAIL YOU JUST SENT.
>
> I RECOMMEND SETTING UP YOUR E-MAIL TO DELAY SENDING ITEMS UNTIL YOU CLICK **SEND/RECEIVE.**
>
> IN MICROSOFT OUTLOOK, YOU GO TO **TOOLS, OPTIONS,** AND CHOOSE **MAIL SETUP.** UNDER **MAIL SETUP,** YOU'LL FIND **SEND/RECEIVE.** REMOVE THE CHECK FROM THE **SEND IMMEDI-ATELY WHEN CONNECTED** BOX. CLICK **OK.**
>
> TEST IT BEFORE YOU TRUST IT. IF YOU SET YOUR E-MAIL UP THIS WAY, YOUR SENT ITEMS WILL ONLY LEAVE YOUR SENT ITEMS FOLDER WHEN YOU PHYSICALLY CLICK THE **SEND/RECEIVE** BUT-TON. IT'S AN EXTRA STEP, BUT CAN PREVENT SUCH A THING HAP-PENING IN THE FUTURE.

Some e-mail programs have a Recall feature that allows you to recall or replace a message—but only if its recipient also uses Microsoft Outlook and has not read the message or moved it from the inbox to another folder. To do this from the **Mail** window, find the navigation pane on the left side of the Outlook window, and click **Sent Items.** Open the message you want to recall or replace. In the message window, on the **Actions** menu, click **Recall This Message,** then click the **Delete unread copies of this message** circle. To be notified about the success of the recall or replacement for each recipient, select the **Tell me if recall succeeds or fails for each recipient** box. The recipient will get a recall alert message, so be sure to cover your tracks by sending another (innocuous and hopefully work-related) e-mail. You might have just saved your ass.

If the e-mail went out, regardless how it happened, you need to assess the damage and address it immediately. The longer you wait to deal with the problem, the worse it will be when you finally do. In the case of accidentally sending an e-mail to your boss that refers to her as "The TPS Report Nazi," you have some serious sucking up to do. If you know she's received and likely read the e-mail (because you couldn't recall

---

TELL HER YOU'RE **TERRIBLE** AT BEING FUNNY

---

it), don't wait until your boss calls you into her office. Go to her office, sit down, and apologize profusely. Don't cry, wail, panic, or beg her forgiveness. Simply apologize (not for sending the e-mail, but for what you called her), tell her that it was highly unprofessional of you to make the statement, tell her you don't really think she's a TPS Report Nazi, and tell her that you were just trying to be funny. Tell her you're terrible at being funny. Chances are, she's probably going to be as horrified and embarrassed as you are (and don't you feel bad now?), so don't

---

Sincerely apologize **DO IT IMMEDIATELY**

---

drag it out. Assure her you **respect** her and understand that you cannot take back the statement, but you wanted to sincerely apologize. Then leave and spend the next several months trying to win back her trust and respect. It might take some time for her to get over it, but if you're up front about your mistake, she will get over it eventually (although every time she says, "TPS Report," she's going to think of you ... and you'll feel humiliated all over again).

Do the same for a coworker you insulted. Sincerely apologize, do it immediately, and I'd also recommend a nice follow-up gesture, like having a cheesecake delivered to her or giving her a certificate for a massage (but don't do that last step for your boss—it will be seen as sucking up). Or if you sent an "all employee" e-mail, send another explaining that you have a really stupid sense of humor, you're an idiot, and you didn't mean what you just said to sound the way it did.

NEVER, EVER SEND ANYTHING THROUGH E-MAIL THAT YOU WOULDN'T WANT YOUR BOSS TO READ.

And by the way, you should make a new rule: Never, ever send anything through e-mail that you wouldn't want your boss to read. Many companies on networks have access to every single e-mail you've ever sent or received. Send one e-mail like this, and it's really easy for your boss to obtain access to every e-mail you sent in the past year—and you might not like the results of that exploratory meeting.

OFFICE DRUNK

When I was in my twenties, I thought the free booze was the best thing about office parties. One company I worked for had an annual holiday blowout with an open bar and taxi service for overserved employees. Taxi service solves the drunk-driving problem (it's a liability for companies to serve liquor at parties without providing an alternate method of transportation), but no one told me my post-work-party hangover would include an entire day of, "Oh shit, what did I say and to whom did I say it?"

I have done the following while intoxicated at office parties: Told a coworker his girlfriend was as dumb as a box of

The easiest way out is to

PLAY GOOD SPORT

hair. Made out with a guy I barely knew from the IT department in the lobby of the hotel where our holiday party was being held, in full view of a mezzanine that held no less than fifty fellow employees. Sat on the lap of a married coworker before I realized his (very angry) wife was sitting right next to him. Cried drunkenly in the high-traffic women's restroom because the guy I had a crush on brought a stunningly beautiful date to the party. I have witnessed the following from intoxicated coworkers: Full frontal nudity after declaring, "I'm not wearing panties!" and flipping her dress over her head. Vomiting on the sidewalk on her knees in front of a very nice hotel, right under the awning where everyone exited. A female coworker slapping a male coworker across the face after he put his hand up her dress without invitation (OK, that one was me, but it was his fault and he deserved it).

On the first work day after the holiday party, no one talks about anything else except the girl who was puking in the street, crying in the bathroom, or making out with the geeky guy from IT. **Do you really want to be that girl?** If you already are, and I'm speaking from the heart here, the best thing to do is keep your chin up and ignore it until it goes away. Everyone understands drunken stupidity. It's fun to talk about who did what, but they'll get tired of it eventually. If you're being teased or mocked, the easiest way out is to play good sport. "You're right, I'm such an ass. How embarrassing for me!" Have a sense of humor about it. We've all been there. Plus, if you immediately acknowledge your bad behavior by poking fun at yourself, you take the fun out of it for everyone who would like to mock the Sidewalk Puking Girl for all eternity.

In the case of insulting someone, such as the coworker whose girlfriend I actually really liked once I got past her mind-numbing stupidity, you should directly address that person and explain that you say really inappropriate things when you've been drinking and you think his girlfriend is fabulous and not stupid at all. Tell him you were just jealous because they seem to have such a great relationship and you're all single and bitter and bitchy. Ask for his forgiveness. That's what I did. In the case of the married coworker/lap/angry wife situation, I apologized to the coworker (who was apparently so drunk himself he didn't seem to mind at all) and asked if I could do anything to assuage his wife's anger.

Let me add here: One incident at a holiday party does not a bad **reputation** make. Two raises a little more concern. Three, and you might have to start thinking about whether or not you want to advance in your career or be the office party girl. Yes, being the office party girl can be a lot more fun, but I was more interested in my paycheck than doing Purple Hooter Shooters with people I worked with. I grew up a little, learned how to eat dinner *before* I started drinking, and limited my office party alcohol consumption to two drinks.

Excelling at your job can go a long way toward recovering your reputation at work. Had I not been the committed, high-work ethic, never-calling-in-sick employee that I was, I'm sure the mistakes I made would have been more damaging to my reputation in the long term. Bosses (and fellow employees) are more inclined to overlook the occasional slipup if you're good at your job.

> **TIP:** NO MATTER WHAT THE SITUATION, OWNING YOUR MISTAKES IS THE FIRST STEP TO OVERCOMING THEM.

CHAPTER SEVEN

MIND THE GAP AND SETTLING UP

Women's annual earnings, relative to men's, have moved up more slowly since the early 1990s than during the 1980s and still remain substantially below parity.

Women who work full-time throughout the year (the usual group used for measuring the gender wage ratio) earned 76.5 percent as much as men in 2004. If part-time and part-year workers were included, the ratio would be much lower, as women are more likely than men to work these reduced schedules in order to manage child rearing and other caregiving work.

In 2004 median annual earnings for women working full-time year-round were $31,223. Men with similar work effort earned $40,798.

(Institute for Women's Policy Research, April 2006, *www.iwpr.org*)

Is it possible that women earn approximately 70 percent of what their male colleagues are making because we are reluctant to discuss financial matters? What do men know that we don't? How are you supposed to feel about getting paid less for the same work? Martyrs and victims don't get raises, so forget about your feelings and start taking action. Stop being afraid to ask for that raise or promotion. Find out what you should be doing to get one, the tools and tips on how to find out if your salary is fair, what your legal and/or personal options are, and how to overcome what stands in your way. There are many ways to ask for a raise, and none of them start with "Um...."

WORK LESS, MAKE MORE MONEY

My best friend of more than ten years—we've known each other since college—is a "radio personality." We both were communications majors; I took the writing road and she went into broadcast journalism. Over the years we've shared all of our major accomplishments, setbacks, wins, and losses. Radio, for those who might not know the field, isn't the most stable industry—not like, say, financial services or nursing. Print journalism doesn't offer much more stability, but the opportunities for advancement and higher-paying jobs are slightly higher than in radio. Nevertheless, my friend loves her work. She was born to be in radio. She has got the voice and the personality for it, loves music, loves to interact with people, and can't imagine doing anything else for a living. As a result she's been in several positions at various radio stations doing the

THERE ARE MANY WAYS TO ASK FOR A RAISE,
AND NONE OF THEM START WITH
"Um . . ."

job of three people (on air, program director, and marketing director in different iterations). When she works for a station, she commits fully—meaning that she is often on the verge of burnout from sixty- and seventy-hour workweeks. A couple of years ago, she had the highest-rated morning show in town and was also doing the job of program director (despite the fact that the station had a program director), along with marketing and promotions. One night she called me to tell me she was thinking about getting out. We'd had similar conversations before, but for the first time in years, I heard a weariness in her voice that hadn't been there in a long time.

Her situation at work was not a good one. She was clearly being taken advantage of, being paid a disc jockey's salary for about three times the work, not to mention that she was making less than the male jocks at the station whose shows weren't even rated as high as hers. If she'd been right in front of me, I would have grabbed her shoulders, shook her, and yelled, "Fight!" Instead I just said, "Don't walk away until you've done everything in your power to make it right. Even if it doesn't work for you, maybe you'll make a difference for the next woman who comes along. Fight for her, even if you don't want to do it for you right now."

"I could teach," she said. She loves kids and used to work with developmentally challenged students as a student teacher.

She could do that, I agreed, but it wouldn't be what she loved. We talked through her options, and she came up with the brilliant idea to sit down with the station manager and put it all out on the table, professionally and honestly. We role-played a couple of different scenarios based on what we thought her boss's reaction would be. She had a reasonable salary increase in mind, along with a request to relinquish her program directing duties to the actual program director who was being paid for the work my friend did on the side. When we hung up, she was fired up, confident, and ready to go for it.

I'd predicted several possible outcomes, but what actually occurred was beyond anything I could have imagined. She called me after the meeting with her boss to give me a rundown. "So I put it all out there—explained that I should be making this much for working these hours, that my show being the highest rated at the least entitled me to make as much as the male jocks, etc.," she said. And how did her boss react? With sympathy and phrases like, "I hear you" and "You're right about that." And then he told her to get her pen and paper ready because he was going to tell her something that would help her out. "Write this down," he said. "Ready?" She was, pen poised, waiting for his sage advice (or his acquiescence to her raise request).

"Work less, make more money," said her boss. "Write that down. Work less, make more money."

"That's why I'm here," said my friend, as she wrote it down.

"Right. That's your new mantra. Work less, make more money. It worked for me." And he showed her the door.

I was stunned, outraged on her behalf, and wanted to jump up and down on this guy's desk and show him where he could put his "mantra." Did she react like I wanted to? No. She handled it with grace and **professionalism,** left his office, and immediately called three contacts and put the word out that she was on the market. It didn't take long for a DJ with a top morning show to get another offer— one for twice what she'd been making at her current station but for working fewer hours. And it included health benefits. She didn't even have to think about it. The following day she stopped by her boss's office to give her notice. He was outraged. He felt betrayed. "After all this station has done for you, etc., etc."

> DON'T WALK AWAY UNTIL YOU'VE DONE EVERYTHING IN YOUR POWER TO MAKE IT RIGHT.

She showed him the pad on which she'd written the "mantra" he had given her just a few days before. "I'm just taking your advice, dude." And she left. (They didn't ask her to work the two weeks' notice she offered.) She's happy in her new job, doesn't have to worry about paying bills or what she'd do if she got sick, and actually works about forty hours a week, just like a regular person.

work less, make more money

mantra

The moral of the story: Salary negotiation doesn't always work on the job that you have, but a higher salary is always worth fighting for. Chances are the next female jock the station hires will be on scale with her male counterparts. More important, my friend has the respect (in the form of a living wage) that makes it all worthwhile. And she gets to continue to do what she loves to do. There's always a way—it might happen where you are now, but if you eliminate giving up as an option, it comes to you.

WHY WOMEN DON'T ASK

1. It might offend my boss. Remember: Work is not about *feelings*. Talking about money makes us uncomfortable. It makes most people uncomfortable. Women, especially, are brought up to believe that discussing money (and one's age) is rude. But in order to close the wage gap (in general and yours specifically), try to see it as a necessary evil.

2. I shouldn't have to ask. "I do a good job," you say. No, you shouldn't have to ask. But put your boss's shoes on for just a sec. Have you told him you're doing a good job? Does he have ESP? Does he know you want to move up in the company? If the answer is no to any of the above, you're going to have to tell him—and ask for the raise. In most companies upper management isn't entirely tuned in to the accomplishments of every single staffer. Managers are often very focused on the bottom line as a whole, not on individual employees. It's up to you to determine what your contribution has been and help him understand your impact on that bottom line.

3. I might get a no. Yes, the answer might be no. There are several reasons your boss could offer up for why you're not eligible for a raise. One might be that the money isn't there. But by asking, when the money is there, your boss will be aware that you're first in line. And by asking, you can also prompt your boss to ensure money is included in the next budget plan for your raise.

YOU'RE TOLD THE MONEY ISN'T THERE

How do you know if the money really isn't there?
Public companies have to file reports to the SEC (the U.S. Securities and Exchange Commission). These reports become public information and are accessible to the public for free, whether you're an employee or not. You can access them via a database called EDGAR (Electronic Data Gathering and Retrieval) at the SEC Web site, *www.sec.gov.* If you're not familiar with company financial reporting, take the site's quick tutorial on how to use EDGAR. By viewing your company's recent reports, you can get a handle on how well the company is doing financially. If your boss said the money isn't there, but the reports indicate otherwise, it doesn't mean you should run back into your boss's office, clutching a handful of reports printed out from the Internet, and call him a liar. Knowledge is power. Ask your boss to explain how your department's budget is structured, ask how often budget planning occurs (some companies operate on calendar year, some on fiscal years beginning in June, and others quarterly), and ask what would need to happen in order to ensure that your raise is included in the next budget.

Knowledge is  **POWER!**

Unlike public companies, private companies are not required to file with the SEC, so the information that can be found in those documents is not necessarily available for private companies. It requires a bit more creativity, but you can still get some answers. Dun & Bradstreet, a publisher that actively seeks financial information from private companies, keeps records of their findings available to the public on its Web site, *www.dnb.com*. Keep in mind that most of the information in these reports was provided voluntarily and is not checked by a government agency. Additionally, there is a fee for viewing many of the available reports. However, don't underestimate the power of the Internet. Even private firms disclose a certain amount of information (in some states, they legally must do so). NASS (the National Association of Secretaries of State) has a link menu to each state's own site at *www.nass.org/sos/sos.html*. If your state requires filings from LLCs (limited liability companies) or other business filings, you'll find them there.

If the company really isn't doing well, this might be a good time to "investigate your options" (meaning: Update your résumé, start networking like hell, and plan an exit strategy).

YOU'RE TOLD YOU DON'T DESERVE A RAISE

If your boss says "no" because you're not doing your job or living up to your full potential, it's a perfect opportunity to ask for specifics on what you can do to improve, get specific goals, discuss areas for development or training, and plan your next step. Don't look at it as a negative. It's important to set yourself up so a **no** will be impossible next time. Sure, you feel like you're doing a fabulous job, your boss is a total asshole who wouldn't know a good employee if she was sitting in his lap (don't even think about it), and you and I both know you're "living up to your full potential." But don't walk away.

Your next move should be to create a checklist of the things your boss cited as needing improvement. Follow up after your "no" meeting with an e-mail that lists your new goals and what you intend to do to make them happen. Send updates on these goals, adding new ones as necessary, every thirty days. After six months schedule another meeting with your boss to check in and repeat your request for a raise. Repeat the process as long as you can stand it—until it either becomes clear you're getting the runaround or your boss is embarrassed into paying you what you're worth. Either way, you get clarity and can decide where to go from here.

You don't always have to whip out the big guns. Simply asking for a raise indicates that you are aware you are worth more than you're being paid.

NEGOTIATE.

YOU GOT A RAISE, IT JUST ISN'T AS MUCH AS YOU EXPECTED

Find out what the average raise is within your company. This isn't difficult—usually a quick call to your company's HR manager will get you an answer. You're not asking for specific salary information on an employee; you're just asking what the average raise is. Depending on the industry and other economic factors (like the state of our national economy or the economy in your state), this figure can vary wildly. I've worked for companies where the average is 6 percent, during the Internet boom when it skyrocketed to 10 to 20 percent, and at mid-level companies with a conservative 3 percent average. NOTE: If you're an above-average employee (which I assume you are since you're reading this book), you should shoot for slightly higher than the average percentage.

NEGOTIATE.

> **TIP:** THE BEST TIME TO ASK ABOUT THE AVERAGE RAISE PERCENTAGE IS DURING YOUR INTERVIEW, RIGHT AROUND THE TIME YOU ASK ABOUT THE COMPANY'S BENEFITS.

Negotiating means that you have to find the balance between slightly higher and ridiculously high. If your company says its average raises are around 2 to 3 percent and you're armed to the teeth with glowing reviews, goal updates, and reports about how much revenue you brought (directly or indirectly) in this year, then asking for a 10 percent raise isn't out of the norm. Most companies recognize that **talent** (sometimes you have to point it out) is worth retaining, which means they have to pay for it. You have to be comfortable with what you're asking for and confident that your contribution to the company is worth it. If you did the minimum to get by, be prepared to accept the minimum. If you went way above and beyond, you'd better have documented every single thing and none of it should be a surprise to your boss.

YOU HAVE TO BE COMFORTABLE WITH WHAT YOU'RE ASKING FOR AND CONFIDENT THAT YOUR CONTRIBUTION TO THE COMPANY IS WORTH IT.

Some women are uncomfortable with even using the word *negotiate*. These are the same women who negotiate every day; they just don't realize it. We negotiate with our spouses about who will do what chore or pick up the kids from soccer practice. We negotiate with friends about which restaurant to meet at, with our kids about their homework, and with family when the "whose house we're visiting for the holidays" conversations begin. We negotiate when we buy cars, sell houses, get divorces, ask for retail discounts when buttons are missing, and try to talk our way out of a speeding ticket. Some people do have more innate ability to negotiate, but none of us are born with the negotiating skills of Henry Kissinger (who negotiated the Paris Peace

NEGOTIATING is a *skill* that must be *learned & practiced.*

Accords in 1973 that effectively ended the Vietnam War, for those of you who slept during World History). Negotiating is a skill that must be learned and practiced. People who claim to be poor negotiators probably just haven't been given the opportunity to give it a go.

NEGOTIATING TIPS-101

Keep your feelings in check. No crying, yelling, or complaining about how much you're in debt. This isn't personal, and making it so isn't going to get you anywhere.

Pretend you don't need it. It sucks, but it is a reality that people who need money the least tend to be the ones who get it. Why? Probably because they have nothing to lose. If you don't get the raise you ask for, you might not be able to swing your rent, pay off your student loans (ever!), or finally stop living paycheck to paycheck. That's going to make you nervous. One of the best negotiating tactics is to forget that you need the money, forget that you have bills to pay, forget that you even need the job. Pretend like you're independently wealthy and you work because you don't have anything better to do—or, better yet, you work because you love the challenge.

You: "This isn't a huge deal, but I was expecting a slightly higher raise."

The likely response: "Oh? How much were you expecting?"

"This much."

"Based on?"

"My work here has been exemplary, I've taken on X, Y, and Z (and sometimes W), and I know you're aware that I am now managing a staff of ten people."

The best response: "Done." (Handshake, everyone's happy).

What you're likely to get: "Well, our budget is this much; our average raises are this much . . ."

Your response: "I understand your average raise is this much, but we both know I'm an above-average employee."

Hopefully you'll provide an out for your boss to do some fancy figuring, and he'll get back to you with a new figure. If not, this is the time to ask how you get from point A (your current raise) to point B (the salary you think you should be making). It might mean taking on additional responsibility, specific goals like bringing in new accounts, changing departments, and so on. Be prepared to follow-through.

Consider perks. If budget is an issue, there are creative ways to be compensated that don't involve an increase in salary. When I worked for a small newspaper with a small budget for editorial salaries, I worked out a few different agreements by which they paid for my cell phone (they had a company account), paid for my personal trainer (they worked with him on advertising trade—and a healthy employee is a happy employee, which is exactly what I told my boss), included a budget item for education so I could attend workshops and conferences annually, and added a few other benefits.

If you hit a brick wall when it comes to the company budget, consider asking for perks like additional vacation time, half-day workdays on Friday, working from home on specific days of the week (we can all telecommute, and it saves on gas and travel time), or education reimbursement. Think long term—education is a great perk, because it's one more thing you can add to your résumé. If you use your cell phone at all for company use (meaning your boss has the number and can reach you on it . . . and does), you should encourage the company to pay for it. I threatened to have mine shut off because I used it for work almost daily and seldom for personal use; the company provided me with one.

POINT A
(YOUR CURRENT RAISE)

THINK LONG TERM

My philosophy is this: If they want to reach you, the method is their fiscal responsibility. It's not about arrogance. If the company genuinely cannot afford to pay you more, they will likely be grateful for the **opportunity** to work with you to figure out what they can do to keep you happy (and keep you as an employee). You have to walk the fine line here—if you consistently use up all of your sick days, are often late to work, and contribute the bare minimum to keep your job, I'd advise against asking for a raise at all, much less trying to negotiate perks.

> *"Toughness doesn't have to come in a* PINSTRIPE *suit."*
>
> ~ DIANNE FEINSTEIN

TIPS FOR THE NEGOTIATING-PHOBIC

You're nonconfrontational. You're a competent, good-at-your-job beta personality type. Talking about money makes you literally sick to your stomach. You'd rather eat Ramen noodles for dinner four nights a week than ask for a raise. So you're scared—that doesn't mean you get off easy. Being successful means feeling the fear and doing it anyway. (Yes, that last line is from self-help author Susan Jeffers. Don't hate me.)

GIVE YOURSELF A GOOD TALKING TO.

Be prepared with a list of reasons why you deserve a raise, but get rid of any chip that might be riding on your shoulder. Forget about the past and look forward. Realize that, regardless the outcome, this is good experience for you.

MIND THE GAP AND SETTLING UP

BE YOURSELF.

If your image of a good negotiator is someone who pounds the table with fists or is a master manipulator, change the image. A good negotiator is passionate, but calm. You can be both soft-spoken and still take a firm position on what you're asking for. If you believe in yourself and that you warrant a higher salary, then just being you (but a you who is asking for more money) is the best tactic you can use. If you try to fit yourself into a mold of what you imagine a good negotiator should be, you will lose authenticity along with credibility.

DON'T BE AFRAID TO ASK QUESTIONS.

If you're dealing with a master negotiator and you know you might be out of your league, forget about your lack of skills in this area. One of the things that women are great at is building relationships. It's harder for someone to say "no" if they know and respect you. One of the ways to earn respect is to be up front and say, "I haven't done this a lot. How would you recommend I get from my current salary to where I would like to be?" Use it as a learning opportunity.

DON'T TAKE IT PERSONALLY.

A **"no"** doesn't mean **no forever** or **no way in hell.** When you realize that the no is about business and not about you personally, it's a lot easier to find out how to get from no to maybe (or even to yes).

PRETEND YOU'RE NEGOTIATING
FOR SOMEONE ELSE.

Some women who fear negotiating are often quite good at it when they're doing so on behalf of a person or organization other than themselves. Think about the times in your life when you've helped raise money for a nonprofit—the negotiating and asking wasn't so hard when it was for a good cause, was it? *You* are a good cause, but if it helps, pretend you're asking for a raise for someone you care about, for your favorite charity, or one of your children.

GETTING YOUR LAW ON

Let's just say you know there is a disparity between your salary and the salaries of male employees performing the same job. It doesn't matter how you found out—people talk, someone might have slipped up, or perhaps it's clear because your male coworkers are driving cars that cost twice what your annual salary is while you're still making due with your breaks-down-every-1,000-miles used car that you've been driving since college. If you suspect that gender might be an issue, it's time to become familiar with the federal laws that protect your rights.

"The TEST for whether or not you can hold a job should not be the arrangement of your CHROMOSOMES."

~ BELLA ABZUG

EQUAL PAY AND COMPENSATION DISCRIMINATION

The right of employees to be free from discrimination in their compensation is protected under several federal laws, including the following enforced by the EEOC: the Equal Pay Act of 1963, Title VII of the Civil Rights Act of 1964, the Age Discrimination in Employment Act of 1967, and Title I of the Americans with Disabilities Act of 1990.

The Equal Pay Act requires that men and women be given equal pay for equal work in the same establishment. The jobs need not be identical, but they must be substantially equal. It is job content, not job titles, that determines whether jobs are substantially equal. Specifically, the EPA provides the following: **Employers may not pay unequal wages to men and women who perform jobs that require substantially equal skill, effort, and responsibility, and that are performed under similar working conditions within the same establishment.**

Each of these factors is summarized below:

Skill: Measured by factors such as the experience, ability, education, and training required to perform the job. The key issue is what skills are required for the job, not what skills the individual employees may have. For example, two bookkeeping jobs could be considered equal under the EPA even if one of the jobholders has a master's degree in physics, because that degree would not be required for the job.

Effort: The amount of physical or mental exertion needed to perform the job. For example, suppose that men and women work side by side on a line assembling machine parts. The person at the end of the line must also lift the assembled product as he or she completes the work and place it on a board. That job requires more effort than the other assembly line jobs if the extra effort of lifting the assembled product off the line is substantial and is a regular part of the job. As a result, it would not be a violation to pay that person more, regardless of whether the job is held by a man or a woman.

Responsibility: The degree of accountability required in performing the job. For example, a salesperson who is delegated the duty of determining whether to accept customers' personal checks has more responsibility than other salespeople. On the other hand, a minor difference in responsibility, such as turning out the lights at the end of the day, would not justify a pay differential.

Working Conditions: This encompasses the additional stress of two factors: (1) physical surroundings such as temperature, fumes, and ventilation; and (2) hazards.

Establishment: The prohibition against compensation discrimination under the EPA applies only to jobs within an establishment. An establishment is a distinct physical place of business rather than an entire business or enterprise consisting of several places of business, so people in the New York branch may make more for the same job than those in Portland and not be subject to a complaint. However, in some circumstances, physically separate places of business can be treated as one establishment. For example, if a central administrative unit hires employees, sets their compensation, and assigns them to work locations, the separate work sites can be considered part of one establishment.

Pay differentials are permitted when they are based on seniority, merit, quantity or quality of production, or a factor other than sex. These are known as "affirmative defenses," and it is the employer's burden to prove that they apply. In correcting a pay differential, no employee's pay may be reduced. Instead the pay of the lower paid employee(s) must be increased.

~ *Source: U.S. Equal Employment Opportunity Commission*

The bottom line: There is recourse if you can prove that the only reason your male counterparts are making more money is because they are male (or "heads of households" or whatever line your boss wants to lay on you). We can't all afford to just walk away from a job, but if you're hitting a wall in the raise department and you know discrimination is taking place, you're probably already looking. If you don't do it for yourself, do it for the other women who might take your place—and file a complaint with the EEOC.

And if you think the system won't work for you, consider this: In 2006 the EEOC received 663 charges of compensation discrimination. That same year, the EEOC resolved 743 compensation discrimination charges and recovered $3.1 million in monetary benefits for charging parties and other aggrieved individuals (not including monetary benefits obtained through litigation).

IF YOU'RE COPING WITH DISCRIMINATION, SEXUAL HARASS-MENT, PROBLEMS WITH FAMILY/MEDICAL LEAVE, OR OTHER GENDER-RELATED EMPLOYMENT ISSUES, DON'T TRY TO GO IT ALONE. THE ERA HAS A HOTLINE STAFFED BY VOLUNTEER COUNSELORS WHO CAN HELP: **800-839-4ERA.**

CHAPTER EIGHT

ONE OF THE GUYS

Many women are hesitant to identify themselves as a feminist because of the negative connotations and stereotypes the word carries—like *man hater* or (my least favorite) *feminazi.* It's easy for people who would welcome a return to the 1950s (women in the kitchen, not the boardroom) to dismiss our ideals and values as feminist propaganda.

But it's important to be clear about one thing:
Being a good feminist has nothing to do with hating men.

It's about equality.
We don't want more; we just want the same.

However, many of today's workplaces are male-dominated on the management side, and women are often accused of "not playing the game" when we question policies or voice concerns. Some women overcome this by overlooking a lack of respect and becoming "one of the guys." We don't have to bury our gender to get ahead. Too often women are outnumbered by stern father figure or frat boy management types. You don't have to be one of the guys to get a foothold on the corporate ladder; in fact, it's not that hard to rise up that ladder. (And no, the answer isn't waiting for the old ones to die off or the young ones to have a fatal keg stand mishap.) What the boys know that you don't is how to garner respect without taking the biggest one out with a sucker punch. It is an office, after all—not a prison.

The days of the "Good Old Boys" network are numbered. In today's world it seems completely insane that there was ever a time when women were "supposed to" stay at home and keep house and care for the offspring, while men brought home the bacon. There are too many single mothers out there for this to be the norm, the divorce rate is sky-high, and women no longer go to college simply to earn their "MRS" degree. We've made a lot of headway in the women's movement. So why are we still facing discrimination, the glass ceiling, and a very masculine Fortune 500 list of CEOs?

"When a woman behaves like a man, why doesn't she behave like a NICE man?"

~ EDITH EVANS

I suspect a lot of today's workplace discrimination has to do with a backlash from the women's movement of the 1970s that resulted in women of the 1980s outfitting themselves in giant shoulder pads, not unlike battle armor; grabbing their Armani briefcases; and infiltrating the moneyed man's world.

Author Danzy Senna writes, "To be a feminist is to be engaged actively in dismantling all oppressive relationships." Feminism isn't about women hating men, or vice versa. It boils down to the haves versus the have nots, the powerful versus the powerless. And like any other diminishing, flawed faction in history, men in leadership positions have every right to worry that the subjugated masses may rise up and kill their "master."

In the 1980s (and early 1990s ... and still in some industries today), women only garnered respect from their male counterparts by acting like they literally had balls. They stormed boardrooms and call centers, left the kids with Mr. Mom, hung their MBAs on their corner office walls, and basically cut the throats of anyone who dared question their authority. Not that I think any of this is a bad thing; it just might have contributed to a slightly off-kilter reputation that women have when they're in high-ranking positions in the corporate world.

Drew Gilpin Faust was about sixty years old when she became the first woman president of Harvard Uni- versity in 2007. She was quoted in a newspaper article as saying that she could hardly have imagined reaching such height when she was a child growing up in a tradition-bound family in the Shenandoah Valley of Virginia. In fact, Faust says, her mother used to tell her: "It's a man's world, sweetie. And the sooner you learn that, the better off you'll be."

Fortunately times have changed. Men of this generation had mothers in the workforce, went to school with women, and grew up with women in the workplace, and they are more likely to understand and identify with women's career aspi- rations and experiences.

> *"We aim to give a* WAKE-UP *call to businesses,*
> *to alert them to the fact*
> *that the next fair-haired boy of their organization*
> *just might be a woman."*
>
> ~ ELIZABETH DOLE, U.S. SENATOR (R-NORTH CAROLINA)

> YOU DO NOT
> HAVE TO ACT
> LIKE A **MAN**
> TO GET AHEAD
> AT WORK.

At the risk of being repetitive, I'll say again that you do not have to act like a man to get ahead at work. But that doesn't mean you can't learn from them. Besides being more comfortable with certain facets of the corporate world, like discussing salary increases and not letting their emotions interfere with their work lives, there are several things that men do in the workplace that women do not.

There were men-only networking groups long before women thought of forming their own—this includes golf courses women can only join if their husbands are also members (and yacht clubs and sports clubs). Men also tend to keep up with contacts involving political affiliation, college alumni, or social groups that date back to college or the early days of their career. Men are more comfortable picking up the phone and asking a college buddy for a favor—like scoring them a job interview for a high-ranking position, giving them a few sales contacts, or asking them to sponsor a club membership. Women often "don't like to impose" on friends and are more

SINGLE WOMEN are often left out of the social networking scene.

hesitant to reach out and make those contacts. Single women are often left out of the social networking scene entirely. Here are some things you can consider:

Network. Personally I despise formal networking events. I can't tell you how many of these I've been to that consist of women running around the room shoving their business cards into the hands of as many people they can make contact with.

There's often little genuine socializing, and I feel like I'm being circled by sharks (or that I'm doing the circling). I do believe in **networking** as a principle. I think it is especially important for women to reach out to other women, but don't discount networking groups that involve both sexes: Many cities have young professional social groups.

Volunteer opportunities are valuable for meeting other people in business, and you can give back to the community at the same time. Offer to sit on the board of a charity, plan events, or help with a fund drive. Mentoring programs are great, because the other mentors are typically going to be other professionals like you. Anywhere you might meet people is a networking opportunity—if you're sincere. Being sincere doesn't mean pushing your business card under their noses and asking what they can do for you. It means developing genuine professional relationships that progress over time. I've met people with whom I've forged ongoing, long-term professional acquaintanceships, people who I can call for advice, for

> YOU DO NOT HAVE TO ACT LIKE A **MAN** TO GET AHEAD AT WORK.

contacts, or just to get a different perspective on something I might be dealing with at work. Networking got me a newspaper job, several leads for freelance writing, and a wealth of information about other industries—all just from casual conversation. Women are great at using personal interaction to build relationships; chatting is never a waste of time.

Offer criticism. Women are often less inclined to offer unsolicited opinions in the business world, because we're afraid we'll be seen as opinionated. Opinions, ladies, are not bad things to have. We tend to think that people will take criticism personally or that they will be offended. I've worked with women who are afraid to speak up in meetings or offer feedback, and they come across as unenthusiastic, less than creative, and wishy-washy. But being able to phrase criticism in a nonconfrontational manner is key to being able to move up the corporate ladder. When offering criticism, criticize the work, not the worker. Cite concrete examples, not feelings.

Be decisive. As I've said before, getting ahead at work is all about taking risks. Women tend to like to mull things over and discuss them before making a judgment call. At a fast-paced company, or one that is built around deadlines, that's not going to fly. Sometimes you have to go with your gut and make an instant decision. Do what you think is right and deal with the consequences later. That doesn't mean you won't allow others to express their opinions and offer suggestions—an employee that can foster a team approach to problem solving is invaluable—but it does mean that someone has to be the one to make the call. If you want to get ahead, that someone should be you.

> OPINIONS, LADIES, ARE NOT BAD THINGS TO HAVE.

Compete. Again, men are raised to do this from Little League on. Women want to foster collaborative work environments where everyone gets along and we're all friends. Nothing wrong with that, but if we refuse to compete we're going to be left in the cold. Competition, contrary to popular belief, doesn't involve backstabbing, manipulation, or throwing one of your coworkers under the bus (figuratively speaking, of course). Competition means that you strive every day to be better at your job than you were the day before, competing with your own best record, as well as letting a coworker's talent or success motivate you to be even better.

> YOU DO NOT HAVE TO ACT LIKE A **MAN** TO GET AHEAD AT WORK.

WHAT WOMEN DO THAT MEN DON'T

There are many things that seem to be built into our nature as women—like cultivating relationships—that can contribute to our success in the corporate world, including the following:

Taking time to talk. Women form different work relationships than men do. We talk about our lives and relate to one another. We know each other's children's names, what schools they attend, what we like to watch on television, and our insecurities. I think it's important to keep most of our personal lives personal, but a big part of building strong working relationships is the investment we make in one another. It doesn't mean you have to talk about the details of the guy you've been crushing on, or spend an hour every morning

COMPETITION MEANS THAT YOU **STRIVE EVERY DAY** *to be better* AT YOUR JOB THAN YOU WERE THE DAY BEFORE.

recapping last night's episode of *Grey's Anatomy,* but interacting with coworkers is a great way to establish and foster a team environment.

Openness. Women think about the individuals they work with, while men tend to think in the context of groups and sometimes forget that it's important to share information. If your company is considering layoffs, you're probably more inclined to want to share that information earlier rather than later, so the people you work with will be prepared when the other shoe drops. This isn't a bad trait to possess.

WHAT MEN THINK WOMEN DO THAT WE DON'T

Because I happen to work for a women's magazine, I've worked in an office full of women since 2004. Sometimes I do miss working in a mixed-gender environment, and there are men in our corporate office, but I spend every single day in the company of women. Like single-sex education, working in an office full of females eliminates any gender issue that might arise—like who's zoomin' who or the urge to wear heels and full-face makeup every single working day. There have been days when I put my hair in a ponytail, pass a washcloth in the general vicinity of my face, and show up at the office wearing an outfit that very closely resembles something one would sleep in.

All those studies that say women dress up for other women? I don't buy it. In every other office I've worked in, there has been a pretty fair ratio of males to females, and I would have called in sick before I showed up without a shower or even just a couple of swipes of mascara and some lip gloss. Does that make me a bad feminist? I don't think so. I think it

Forget all those myths
ABOUT WORKING IN AN OFFICE FULL OF WOMEN
BEING THE EQUIVALENT OF NAVIGATING
a viper's nest.

means I'm a female and I enjoy male attention. I don't want to date men I work with (and haven't done so since my early twenties). I really don't even care if they think I'm attractive. I just don't feel comfortable showing the worst side of myself—and therefore showing weakness—in a mixed-gender workplace. Working with men kept me on guard. Working in an office full of women means I don't have to be quite as vigilant (though I stick to one of my original decrees: Trust no one).

Forget all those myths about working in an office full of women being the equivalent of navigating a viper's nest. Sure, there are catty women out there who stab other women in the back—but there are men out there who do it too. I've had comments from friends (and even some complete strangers) about how I must have to watch my back, deal with gossip, or referee catfights. I work in one of the most collaborative and supportive environments I've ever experienced in this office full of women. Maybe my situation is unique, but I doubt it.

I'm not suggesting that you run out and try to find a new job in a single-sex work environment, but don't discount it. Don't assume that working with an office full of women is more difficult than working in a male-dominated workplace. When I worked in a coed office, I didn't wear makeup to try and entice my male boss to give me a raise. I showed up clean and tidy and pulled together because I knew if I didn't, I was going to be perceived as weak. In any professional environment, not showing up to work in your pajamas is a good idea if you don't want to be treated like a doormat.

(YOUR) SEX IS NOT A WEAPON

A 2007 study by Tulane University said that women who flirt at work get fewer raises and promotions. The study included 164 female MBA graduates, 49 percent of who said they have tried to advance their careers by sometimes engaging in flirtatious behavior—everything from crossing their legs provocatively to leaning over a table to allow men to look down their shirts. While this embarrasses me on behalf of my sex to no end, it is comforting to know that the percentage who said they engaged in such behavior earned, on average, $50,000 to $75,000 a year. The rest of the survey respondents, who said they did not flirt at work, made an average of $75,000 to $100,000 a year. The study reported that even infrequent flirtatious behavior could be detrimental to career advancement. So if anyone ever advises you to use your "God-given assets" to get ahead at work, ignore them (or if it's your boss talking, document it so you can sue later).

THE BOTTOM LINE: ERASING GENDER DISTINCTION IN THE CORPORATE WORLD WILL ONLY HAPPEN IF BOTH MEN AND WOMEN ACTIVELY WORK TOGETHER TO CHANGE NEGATIVE OR UNHELPFUL PATTERNS.

NOW THAT YOU'RE THE BOSS

So you've won the war and made it to upper or middle management—or even CEO. How can you use your power for good and not evil, creating a productive office environment, making changes to corporate culture from the inside, and juggling work and home lives?

You *can* be a good boss without putting in eighty-hour workweeks; it just takes a little creative planning.

In any job I've ever had, I never really set out to get into management. What drove me to do better and learn more—even when I was waiting tables—is that I wanted to make more money. Waitressing was my first real job. (Actually I started as a hostess, because I was fifteen years old and not old enough to wait tables yet.) I wasn't that great at it and didn't particularly enjoy it, but I wanted to make money so I hustled my tail off. I took every shift offered, even the worst ones ("Kids Eat Free" night was a horror). I rolled silverware, filled ketchup bottles, ran other servers' plates for them, ran the register when it was slow, and did everything else I could to keep my hours and my tips high. And then they offered me a management position. I was in high school.

I'm not telling you this so you'll think I'm so super smart or amazing—I'm not. Even back then, I knew what overtime meant. I also knew that my minimum wage (at the time for a waitress it was $2.35 an hour plus less-than-stellar tips) wasn't going to cut it. So I started training for management. I can't say I loved it, but I did it for a year until my restaurant time started cutting into my study time. (And the regional manager was a psycho former Miss Some Southern State who was expecting way too much of a sixteen-year-old, something I discovered the day she suggested I drop out of school to spend more time working.) So I quit.

Next job, same story. And the one after that. My own work ethic was killing me. I found myself, at twenty-three years old, so burned out that I often didn't know if I was going to survive the workweeks. I was also taking college classes (for

> I'D NEVER ASK AN EMPLOYEE TO DO SOMETHING I HAVEN'T DONE MYSELF.

six years, without even a summer semester off). And I was managing a staff of twenty-odd people. Then I was twenty-four, twenty-five, twenty-six, and I was the boss. I took every workshop the company let me take on management, human resources, and corporate policy making, and I learned a lot. But I actually learned a lot more from the people I had worked for in the past. I'd had enough bad bosses to know what I didn't want to be

and developed my own style based on how I wanted to be managed. I've modified my style over time, but still stick to the same basic principles:

✳ I don't manage people;
I manage a function or a department.

✳ I coach people.

✳ I'm not the kind of person who needs hand-holding; therefore I have trouble with employees who need a lot of it.

I lead by example—which means I'd never ask an employee to do something I haven't done myself. When I was running a call center, word came down from upper management that my staff needed to make forty phone calls a day (outgoing collection calls). I hadn't really been tracking their stats up to that point, so I didn't know if that was possible or not. I spent the following week with an aging (collections) list making phone calls for eight hours a day. My average was fifty calls a day, so I countered the edict from upper management with my higher figure and trained the staff individually on productivity tips (leaving complete info on messages to save on callbacks, giving e-mail addresses when leaving messages

I THINK OUR JOB AS MANAGERS IS TO ENCOURAGE & COACH.

to receive responses via e-mail while still on the phone ... I'm all about multitasking). Within a month I had a staff each making fifty calls every day, and our receivables were down by about forty-five days. I got a big raise that year.

The reason my staff accepted my challenge was because they all knew I had done it myself for a week first (and jumped in whenever needed on an ongoing basis), so I wasn't asking the impossible. I've had too many bosses in the past who just randomly demand things without first considering feasibility. I think our job as managers is to encourage and coach, not insist on setting goals without doing our research first.

I don't have a problem firing someone if it isn't working out. It's sort of a running joke (though not a particularly funny one) in my office that, if someone needs firing, I'm the one to do it. It's not that I enjoy it—if I ever get to the point where I enjoy firing someone, I know it will be time to change careers—it's that the company is more important to me than

the feelings of the people I work with. I know it sounds coun-
terintuitive to some of what you've read in this book, because
I am invested in the people I hire and do work to train and
coach them. But I am also able to recognize when it's time to
cut our losses. And I genuinely believe that's the best thing for
my company and for the person I'm firing (though they might
not have agreed with that at the time). I also happen to be
good at it. I've been in meetings with other managers as a
third-party witness during a termination meeting and learned

If you fire someone on a Friday,
and they show up for work on Monday,
you didn't do it right.

what not to do just by observing. One such meeting dragged
on for almost forty-five minutes, and at the end, the employee
still didn't understand that she was being let go. This is really,
really poor management. If you fire someone on a Friday, and
they show up for work on Monday, you didn't do it right.

BEARER OF BAD NEWS:
LETTING AN EMPLOYEE GO

During a termination meeting (or exit meeting, or
firing, or whatever your company calls it), you should
have documentation on previous performance cita-
tions, reviews, or write-ups or any other information
relevant to the employee's performance on the job.
Unless the employee suddenly violated a single rule
that resulted in his or her firing, you're probably let-

ting him or her go because of ongoing poor performance. If you haven't documented previous discussions, e-mails, or other coaching attempts, then you shouldn't be firing him or her. If the employee is surprised at being fired, then you're not doing your job. In some states (like the one I live in now), you don't actually have to have a reason for letting an employee go—legally. I think it's good business practice and good management to be able to demonstrate that you've made an effort as the employee's manager to do everything in your power to help him or her succeed. Once that's out of the way and off the table, it's time for termination.

✳ You're going to be nervous because you don't know how the employee will react. If you believe he or she may be volatile, have a third party (like your HR manager) present.

✳ You're probably also nervous (or sick to your stomach), because firing someone is painful. If you don't feel this way, you're not human and shouldn't be a manager anyway.

✳ Some people say the best time to fire someone is on a Friday afternoon. I think these people are cowards. I like to consider the employee I'm firing rather than my own convenience, but I do try to schedule termination meetings toward the end of the day to avoid any embarrassment for the employee as he or she packs up personal items. I think firing someone on a Monday allows him or her to begin looking for a job the very next day, while firing someone on a Friday gives him or her a weekend to cry and wallow.

✳ In the meeting, "You're fired" (or a kind version of "You're fired") should be the first or second thing out of your mouth. A sample script: "Hi Jane, have a seat. I'm sorry to tell you that we have to let you go. I know you're aware that it isn't working out. We appreciate your efforts but have decided the best recourse is to terminate your employment effective immediately."

✳ Jane is going to be upset. Jane might even cry (keep a box of tissues in your desk drawer). Jane might even argue her case—do not, under any circumstances, allow that conversation to happen. If you're

---

THE ABSOLUTE **WORST** THING YOU COULD DO FOR BOTH JANE AND YOURSELF (AND YOUR COMPANY) IS TO ALLOW YOURSELF TO BE TALKED INTO GIVING HER **"ONE MORE CHANCE."**

---

having this meeting, you've made up your mind and the absolute worst thing you could do for both Jane and yourself (and your company) is to allow yourself to be talked into giving her "one more chance." Let her cry, let her talk, but don't say anything more than "I'm so sorry."

✳ Once it sinks in, offer to help her pack up her things. Some companies have policies about security or someone from HR standing by. I think it's kinder to have someone (like yourself) actually stand by. The reason? You do not want a freshly terminated employee back at her desk alone to send out one last goodbye e-mail to the **All Employees** e-mail list. You will not like this e-mail. I've seen one or two in my time, and they were ugly.

I'm so sorry.

* No, she cannot log back into her computer. No, she can't e-mail her friend in accounting one last time. No, she cannot take the company files. Only personal things, and it's a good idea to have an empty box ready for just such an occasion.

* You should have worked out details like severance, how she will receive her last check, and who she should contact for COBRA health benefits, should she decide to opt for those. Do not recommend she file for unemployment—your boss will hate you for doing it (unemployment claims are hard on a company's bottom line; ideally the employee you just fired will find another job that suits her better tomorrow).

I've actually scored a few points with bosses who have delegated the unpleasant task to me. I once fired someone after I'd only been on a job for three weeks, and I had to do it by telephone because my boss didn't even want to see her back in the office. Did I love it? No. I did it because—say it with me now: *I wanted to make more money.* A smart boss hires employees who compensate for areas they might not be so great at. Mine hired me because I'm good at being "the bearer of bad news." And I don't mind at all.

"Recognize your gifts
and DELEGATE *the rest."*
~ LYNNE FRANKS

A GOOD BOSS

✳ **Doesn't see a good employee as a threat;** she sees a good employee as an opportunity to plug any existing holes in her management style.

✳ **Expects everyone she hires to be after her job;** otherwise how will she move onward and upward?

✳ **Is honest and accepts honesty from her employees.** I think everyone, in their heart of hearts, knows that shooting the messenger only ensures you won't get any more messages. The truth can be messy, painful, or just plain distasteful. But it can also set you free.

✳ **Delegates.** *Delegate* is just a fancy word for sharing responsibility with others, but it can also be the most difficult thing to do. Almost everyone feels hesitation when giving up certain aspects of his or her job, but you have to be able to do it in order to move up the ladder yourself. Trust your staff to make their own mistakes, and it won't be so hard.

✳ **Sees the big picture.** "Good leadership is about the company's success, not your own," says Anne Mulcahy, Chairman and CEO of Xerox Corporation.

✳ **Is in touch with what her employees do.** My current boss asks for a list of my current responsibilities about every six months. I do the same for anyone working on my team. It's not to create "busy work," it's so we can stay informed on what our employees are handling and what new things they've taken on, and it makes writing performance reviews a heck of a lot easier.

✳ **Treats people with respect.** Bullying and hostility are big, giant no-no's when you're the boss.

✲ **Is sincere and selective.** Don't throw out compliments like dog biscuits—you're not working with a bunch of bitches (I hope). Phrases like "Thanks for your hard work" and "You're a gem" mean a lot more if your employees don't hear them every other week.

✲ **Leads by example.** Don't expect your employees to show up on time every day if you wander in the office midmorning, or whenever you feel like it. You can't institute a one-hour lunch policy if you habitually take two- or three-hour lunches. Do this, and your employees will eventually lose respect for you.

✲ **Focuses on the big picture.** Women sometimes concentrate so much on the tasks at hand that we forget to take a big step back and consider the company as a whole. From time to time we need to change things and see what works best, and the only way to do this is to view it from the outside. If it helps, try explaining your department's workflow to a colleague or someone else who doesn't work for your company. Or create a workflow document. Sometimes just talking or writing it out helps us see things that we cannot on a day-to-day basis.

> *"There is* NO POINT *at which you can say,*
> *'Well, I'm successful now.*
> *I might as well take a nap.'"*
> ~ CARRIE FISHER

It does seem like women have to work twice as hard to receive the same amount of recognition, but don't let that grow into a chip on your shoulder. It's taken us years to change stereotypes about women in the workplace, and we're going to have to continue to work hard—at least as long as the glass ceiling and wage disparity still exist.

There is a misconception that we all have to like our coworkers. We don't. Chances are there will be someone (or several someones) in your career that you simply won't like. But keeping it professional means we do not allow our personal feelings to impact our work environment. Don't help perpetuate the stereotypes by being catty, gossiping, or waiting for the first opportunity to stab the person you don't like in the back. If this person is working for you and he or she is not doing his or her job, let him or her go. If it happens to be your boss, or a colleague, and you don't respect his or her work (or know he or she is not doing his or her job), it should just be

IT DOES SEEM LIKE
WOMEN HAVE TO
WORK TWICE AS HARD
TO RECEIVE THE
SAME AMOUNT OF
RECOGNITION.

IT DOES SEEM LIKE
WOMEN HAVE TO
WORK TWICE AS HARD
TO RECEIVE THE
SAME AMOUNT OF
RECOGNITION.

a matter of time. I always like to stand back, be professional, give a little rope, and let that person hang him- or herself with it. I think if we are manipulative or create drama in the workplace, it will always come back to bite us in the ass.

I'd love to issue a challenge to all women in the working world to at least attempt to move up the corporate ladder, whether you plan on being in it for the long haul or not. Hesitancy can be a career killer; instead of worrying about what might happen five years from now (... master's degree? Kids?), just do for now. In order to make women in management roles commonplace, we have to actually pursue those positions. A recent Gallup poll is on our side with this one. Until the 1980s both men and women clearly preferred men as bosses. But then the tide started shifting. Today nearly 50 percent of adults have no preference. Interestingly, younger men prefer female bosses, while older men say they would rather have a male manager. The latest Gallup survey also found that the younger a woman is, the more likely she is to find a female boss acceptable. I think we can expect big changes in the next ten to twenty years.

GIVING BACK

Once you've made it to management, the best thing you can do to advance both your career and the careers of women in general is to be a mentor. It doesn't have to be through an official mentorship program (though there are some great nonprofits out there for that). You can call your local college and let them know you'd be interested in having a female intern (try women's studies departments). Or look around your own company. Is there a young woman in your department or another area who could benefit from a hand up? Invite her to lunch once a month, talk about work issues (make it a safe haven, be ethical, and don't share her comments with her boss unless you have something positive to say), ask what she needs help with, offer advice. Do for her what you would have liked to have someone do for you back then.

IS THERE A YOUNG WOMAN IN YOUR DEPARTMENT OR ANOTHER AREA WHO COULD BENEFIT FROM A HAND UP?

INVITE HER TO LUNCH.

Mentor

Women need female role models. It's great to read biographies from amazing women like Carly Fiorina or Anita Roddick, but it's even better to have a role model you've actually met in person, someone you work with or see on a regular basis, and someone you can e-mail or call and ask for advice. Marie Quintana, vice president of ethnic sales development for PepsiCo in Dallas, mentors several young women at PepsiCo as part of the company's Women of Color Multicultural Alliance. And since 2001 PepsiCo executives who are women of color have doubled from 72 to 144. In the same period women of color among the company's external directors increased from 7.1 percent to 14.3 percent.

I've had several mentors in my career, most of whom weren't even aware they were serving as such. I have one right now, and she doesn't know it. Because the positive influence of women has had such an impact on my own career, I spend as much time as I can trying to be that for younger women. And I hope I've succeeded.

MOVING ON

Being able to let go of conflict and move forward is key to maintaining professional relationships. We've all been in situations where we were underappreciated (and if you haven't been there yet, consider yourself lucky).

Just because someone has a management title doesn't mean he or she is capable of motivating and inspiring employees.

Before you decide to cut your losses and find another job, make sure you're not the reason that your current job sucks.

I once worked peripherally with a young woman who I would best describe as quietly disgruntled. Like most of us, there were aspects of Quietly Disgruntled's job with which she was not happy. She complained fruitlessly and often to coworkers and friends, including me, but seldom brought up issues of her dissatisfaction with the one person who could make her work life better: her boss.

Since most of us were tired of her frequent litany of complaints, and I happened to be one of the few alphas in the group, the responsibility of encouraging Quietly Disgruntled to take action fell in my lap. After several ineffective attempts to politely steer her in the direction of scheduling a meeting with the boss to discuss her (mostly valid) complaints, I finally asked her to lunch outside of the office, where we could talk freely. If it seems like I may have been overstepping—or going over and above when I could have just ignored her—I was in a situation in which it was quite possible that I would end up managing this person in the future, so it was in my best interest to quash her bitching before I became the object of it.

During lunch we talked about her grievances: It had been more than a year since Quietly Disgruntled's last performance review and raise, she'd been promised a larger work space and computer upgrade several months prior and kept getting "blown off" (her words) by the department in charge of supplying such things, she felt as though her boss didn't respect her work, she believed he was just waiting for her to quit, and so on, and so on, and so on . . .

> SHE SELDOM BROUGHT UP ISSUES OF HER DISSATISFACTION WITH THE ONE PERSON WHO COULD MAKE HER WORK LIFE BETTER:
> HER BOSS.

After asking a few questions (when was the last time she had asked for a review meeting, equipment upgrade, larger office, and so on?), and discovering that it had been quite a while, I gave her my analysis: She lived to bitch. Except I said it in a nicer way—something about her psychological need to resent authority figures combined with a passive-aggressive personality, but I severely sugarcoated the whole thing so she wouldn't cry—or offer up more bitching.

"Do you want my advice?" I asked (even though I was so worn out by almost an hour of speed bitching that I was going to dole it out whether she wanted it or not). "Make a list of your top three issues, make an appointment, dig down deep and find your composure, and calmly talk to your damn boss." I added that it was a good time to discuss things like salary and work environment, but probably not the best time to talk about

her request for four extra vacation days for her honeymoon or how much she hated the receptionist for always announcing her personal calls for the entire office to hear.

Quietly Disgruntled scheduled the appointment, her boss was receptive, and by the end of the month the paperwork was filled out for a raise, she was moved to a larger work area in another area of the building, and her new computer was shipped and delivered. Problem solved, right? Wrong.

Here's where the story gets a little sticky. Even though Quietly Disgruntled was able to cross her top three off her work wish list, she was not able to let go of her seething resentment. It still pissed her off that it took so long to get

IT'S IMPOSSIBLE
TO TURN BACK TIME

what she asked for, plus the simple fact that she had to ask made her feel like her work wasn't being respected. She continued to complain to coworkers about the same issues, a few new ones, and her general dissatisfaction with the way she felt she'd been treated.

Her problem: the inability to let go.

What she should have done: moved on.

How the story ended: I didn't want her on my team after I was promoted, so I offered her the choice of resigning or being let go. And because I'm a nice person (or, at the least, an honest one), I also told her that it would have been in her best interest to accept her victory—it was a victory, after all—and move on. Managers are supposed to be good problem solvers, but it's impossible to turn back time, which is what she really wanted at the root of all her complaining. It reminded me of an early *Mad TV* sketch that involved a man losing his temper in a restaurant, despite every concession he was offered by the waiter and manager. "I know my meal's free, but I wanted it *twenty minutes ago . . .* can you give it to me *twenty minutes ago?* I've been waiting for *twenty minutes!"* as his gratis meal sat in front of him getting cold. The waiter: "Sir, your food is here and it's free and here's a certificate for another meal at a later date." Patron: *"But you can't give it to me twenty minutes ago, can you?"*

I've had some really good bosses, but none who were capable of actually turning back time. When Quietly Disgruntled's problems were solved, it took the wind out of her sails.

ONE OF MY RULES WHEN DEALING WITH A DIFFICULT BOSS:

She no longer had a point of reference for communicating with coworkers. She had to really stretch to think about things to complain about. Yes, her boss was an ass for not acting sooner. Yes, she was probably going to have to be **proactive** about what she wanted forever and ever (or as long as she worked for him). But not being able to move forward is a career killer. She didn't have to

ONCE YOU GET WHAT YOU WANT, NEVER (EVER) MENTION THE CONFLICT AGAIN.

suddenly become her boss's biggest fan, or fall over backwards with gratitude because he finally did what he was supposed to in order to fairly compensate and ensure a productive work environment for one of his employees, but she did have to let it go.

One of my rules when dealing with a difficult boss: Once you get what you want, never (ever) mention the conflict again. Ever. First, if you had to put that much effort into fight-

EVER.

ing a battle, why rehash it over and over? You won or reached a compromise. Celebrate and move on. Second, think about how you would react if you were the boss (or how you will react when you *are* the boss). Suppose you had an issue with an employee—due to an oversight on your part, an accounting error, or simply having way too much on your plate—and you fixed the problem. Would you want that employee to reward what you see as your good boss-like intentions by continuing to bitch about you to anyone who will listen? It doesn't make for good boss-employee collaborative relationships, and even if your boss never catches wind of your constant complaining, your coworkers will eventually either tune it out or distance themselves (if they're smart).

Perhaps you've known a Quietly Disgruntled, Loudly Disgruntled, or a Perpetually Disgruntled at some point in your career. You might even have been disgruntled yourself.

> **WRITE THIS DOWN:** DISGRUNTLED IN ANY FORM IS TOXIC. TOXIC EMPLOYEES CAN KILL BUSINESS. DON'T BE ONE.

MOVING ON, PART DEUX:
WHEN YOU KNOW THE JOB'S NOT GOING TO WORK OUT, AKA "QUITTIN' TIME."

*"If you must play,
decide upon three things at the start:
the* RULES *of the game,
the* STAKES, *and the* QUITTING *time."*

~ CHINESE PROVERB

You've done everything in your power to try to make it work. You're inscrutable. You're motivated. You're talented, hard-working, and haven't taken a sick day in two years. You've had meeting upon meeting with your boss about your salary (or lack thereof) or your work environment, but things aren't getting better. It may not even be a gender issue—chances are slim that you're being singled out because you have a vagina, but you still fought the good feminist fight. You've done your part. Now what?

Most important, don't quit in a fit of pique. Don't let your frustration at not being able to make it work push you into doing something drastic. Unless you're independently wealthy (and I'm assuming you're not since you bought this book), you can't afford to be out of work while you're looking for work.

Pagan Kennedy, one of my favorite authors, wrote in her introduction to *Pagan Kennedy's Living: A Handbook for Maturing Hipsters* about "quitting in place." It was the first time I'd heard the term, defined by Ms. Kennedy as "you pretend to do your work, all the while using the office's phones, faxes and copy machines for your own illicit purposes." While my own work ethic won't allow me to stand behind the idea of ripping an employer off while you decide what to do next, I think a modified version of the concept can work—and it did for me.

I mentally quit my job working for a software company about six months before I actually packed up my desk and trudged through the reception area lugging my box full of six years of accumulated personal items. (It would have been four boxes, had I not had the foresight to start bringing some things home when I mentally quit.) In my six years with the company, I had also attended college year-round in the evenings (and some Saturday morning classes). I did a bit of freelance writing on the side, and my final two years of college courses consisted solely of writing classes. I knew I wanted to write for a living, but I wasn't sure how to get there. The one thing I was sure about? I wanted out of the corporate world.

I wrote the following in one of my notebooks in 1999: *You have an office job. Maybe you just took the job "until something better came along." At first, the job wasn't so bad. You were learning new things, interacting with new people. You thought you would be able to work on your writing evenings and weekends. But now the job has become mundane, boring, and worse, it sucks every drop of creativity right out of you. You leave work, drive home in a fog, and park yourself on the couch in front of the television with a peanut butter and jelly sandwich in one hand and the remote in the other. You can't concentrate long enough to watch a sitcom. You wonder what happened.*

I thought I was writing it as an article pitch to a magazine, but realized I was describing myself. I talked to a few friends and family members who thought I was crazy for considering leaving a high-paying, secure job with great benefits. In my heart I knew I'd be crazy to stay. What had once been

DON'T QUIT IN A FIT OF PIQUE.

challenging bored me to tears. My boss was never going to foster the creative, collaborative environment I craved. Because I was in a management position, my job description had changed

What had once been

CHALLENGING

BORED ME TO TEARS.

from taking on something new every few weeks to spending eight to ten hours a day writing personnel reviews and enforcing policies I didn't particularly agree with. What had once excited and **inspired** me—the company's growth, learning new software programs, revamping my own job description and the departments I managed—left me drained and depressed.

In hindsight I know it wasn't the company's fault; it was mine. I'd spent six years working fifty- and sixty-hour work-weeks, plus attending classes, writing papers, and trying to maintain some semblance of a social life. Once I graduated, I had more time to think about what it was I really wanted—and it wasn't writing up employees for being five minutes late to work. About the same time I began investigating what it would take to build a freelance writing career, I mentally quit my job. I didn't stop doing what was required of me, but I *only* did what was required. I no longer spent late nights doing job-related research on my computer at home. Instead I devoted

I DIDN'T STOP DOING WHAT WAS REQUIRED OF ME, BUT I ONLY DID WHAT WAS REQUIRED.

all my spare time to writing query letters, reaching out to editors, and trying to get some of my writing published so I'd have clips before I actually walked away. It wasn't until I emotionally quit the job that I realized how deeply I'd been invested in the company—a company, when I finally shone that bright light of reality on it, that I really didn't care about at all.

I'm not knocking the company I used to work for. In fact I'm eternally grateful for the lessons I learned (the hard way or otherwise). I probably wouldn't be writing this book if it wasn't for the woman who hired me and continued to have enough faith in me to allow me to advance there. At the time, I was one of only two managers who did not have a college degree, and I was definitely the youngest. It must have taken a lot of patience to set a green, gung-ho, feet-first young woman like me loose to run a department, but my boss did it despite our frequent philosophical conflicts.

During the six months of "quitting in place," I struggled with being able to actually walk away. At my salary, I was living quite comfortably. I was terrified of having to go back to waiting tables or eating Ramen noodles. I was smart enough to have (a) contributed to my company's 401K for the entire length of my employment and (b) saved a little extra money once I decided to leave. And because I was fully vested when I left, my entire retirement fund (including the company's contributions) belonged to me.

In the end, when I finally packed my little box and drove away from that nondescript sand-brick building for the last time, it was because my boss (and her best friend, the HR manager) had discovered my side writing gig. It's a long story, and the standoff lasted three days, but I can best sum it up by saying that I stuck to my guns and refused to resign, and the company now has a policy about moonlighting (having a second job in addition to your main job, something I still believe shouldn't be prohibited), as well as one about severance pay that they probably named after me. I used the same negotiating skills I'd honed during my seven or eight performance reviews to negotiate my way out of my job with what I felt was a fair return on my six-year investment.

I haven't regretted walking away for a single moment. Even when the freelance writing checks were few and far between, even when my health insurance ran out, and even when I desperately missed being able to blow $400 on a pair of shoes, leaving was the right thing for me to do. I know this because I haven't had a stress headache, nighttime teeth grinding, or crying jags in the car on the way home from the office since.

CAREER TRAP

Beware the "golden handcuffs," a profession that pays you so well that you enter into a lifestyle (house, cars, stuff, and more stuff) that traps you. You may end up in a vicious cycle of trying to earn more in order to pay for things you might not really need—or want—in the first place.

MAKING YOUR CASE

If you've had consistent and ongoing on-the-job conflict and plan to file a complaint with the EEOC, **do not quit your job** unless your work environment has become detrimental to your physical or emotional health (see Chapter 7: Mind the Gap and Settling Up)—and even so, don't quit before you have documented proof of one or the other. You will have a better case if your employer terminates your employment, depending on the state in which you live and the reason for termination. Some women worry about having a firing on their "permanent record." If your work situation is such that you have a valid case with the EEOC, termination cannot be a factor when you're seeking future employment. Additionally, in most states, the law specifically outlines what a former employer may disclose to potential employers seeking references on your behalf. In most cases all they are allowed to disclose is your length of employment and whether or not you have "rehire status." I've been fired before and don't consider it a detriment to my career.

COBRA

If you do end up leaving your job before you have another lined up, you should do everything you can to ensure you are covered by health insurance during your unemployment. If your health insurance was covered by your employer, you can participate in COBRA health benefits.

Congress passed the landmark Consolidated Omnibus Budget Reconciliation Act (COBRA) health benefit provision in 1986. COBRA provides certain former employees, retirees, spouses, former spouses, and dependent children the right to temporary continuation of health coverage at group rates. This coverage, however, is only available when coverage is lost due to certain specific events (such as layoffs, forced resignations, or terminations without egregious circumstances). You can also qualify for COBRA if you quit your job, as long as you're not doing so under duress or because you committed an ethical violation. Group health coverage for COBRA participants is usually more expensive than health coverage for active employees. This is because usually the employer pays a part of the premium for active employees, while COBRA participants generally pay the entire premium themselves. COBRA is ordinarily less expensive, though, than individual health coverage.

WHO IS ENTITLED TO BENEFITS UNDER COBRA?

There are three elements to qualifying for COBRA benefits. COBRA establishes specific criteria for plans, qualified beneficiaries, and qualifying events. A qualified beneficiary generally is an employee, the employee's spouse, or the employee's dependent child covered by a group health plan on the day before a qualifying event. Qualifying events are certain events that would cause an individual to lose health coverage. The type of qualifying event will determine who the qualified beneficiaries are and the amount of time that a plan must offer the health coverage to them under COBRA. A plan, at its discretion, may provide longer periods of continuation coverage. Qualifying events for employees include voluntary or involuntary termination of employment for reasons other than gross misconduct and reduction in the number of hours of employment.

~ Source: Department of Labor, www.dol.gov

RULES FOR QUITTING

1. Don't burn your bridges. Even if you don't feel it now, eventually you will look back on this time as a learning experience. And you may want to pelt me with new-age self-help books for this one, but even the worst job is a learning experience. Which brings me to ...

2. Leave gracefully. Never quit without notice, never lose your temper when giving notice, and never use resignation as an opportunity to pop your top and vent all the frustration you've been bottling up in the form of personal insults directed at your boss. If it sounds like I'm a little too familiar with this topic, it's because I've made all the above mistakes.

3. Put it in writing. After you've given verbal notice and outlined the conditions of your final weeks of employment, follow up with a letter (via e-mail is fine) that reiterates your notice. **EXCEPTION:** Do not put anything in writing if you are in the process of filing a complaint with the EEOC, unless the EEOC advises you to do so.

Here is a sample resignation letter:

> *Dear Mr. Boss Man,*
>
> *Effective at the end of two weeks' notice, which begins on [date], I resign my position with this company. I thank you for the opportunities and benefits I have received as an employee and will do everything possible to ensure a smooth transition as I leave the company.*
>
> *Sincerely,*
> *Ms. I Can't Get Outta Here Fast Enough*

DON'T

4. Revenge is never a good idea. No matter how well deserved or how many hours you've spent lying awake at night dreaming about it, resist. No matter how well planned your revenge, there's always the chance that you'll get caught—and if that happens, even if your revenge was completely legal, you've definitely burned a bridge you're never going to be able to rebuild.

I once worked at the same company as a friend who was one of the sweetest women you'd ever meet. She was in another department, and her boss was a walking nightmare, complete with fangs and claws and snakes for hair. My friend tolerated indignity after indignity—with professionalism and grace—for more than four years. She was dumped on, screamed at, publicly humiliated, disparaged (despite being really good at her job), and basically used as her boss's scratching post month after month, yet she still showed up to work every day with a smile on her face and a spring in her step. When my friend finally left the company for a better-paying job, she graciously offered two weeks' notice and to train her replacement. A month or so after her departure, a strange odor began emanating from her former boss's office. I heard about it through another friend who worked in that department, and I couldn't resist checking it out myself. (At this point my friend's former boss had temporarily relocated to a conference room until the source of the smell could be located.) It was hard to describe—the closest comparison I could make was that it smelled like a combination of low tide and paper mill. And it was God-awful. The odor was so bad that you couldn't actually stand inside

> NO MATTER HOW WELL PLANNED YOUR REVENGE, THERE'S ALWAYS THE CHANCE THAT YOU'LL GET CAUGHT.

the office; it was plenty strong several feet from the doorway. They'd tried to find the source for weeks, even bringing in experts in carpet cleaning and mold detection, and completely replaced the carpet in the office.

Because I was still in touch with my friend (who loved her new job, by the way), I mentioned it to her over the phone. I knew she'd believe, as I did, that Karma was getting even on her behalf. But my friend (who will forever remain anonymous because she swore me to secrecy forever and ever . . . and I always keep those sacred promises) laughed until she choked as she told me about her revenge. She'd gone into her boss's office the day before her last day at work, unscrewed the base of her boss's expensive ergonomic chair, filled the hollow core with raw fresh shrimp, and reassembled the chair. It took a few weeks before the smell was detectable, but it got so bad so quickly that it was impossible to tell where it was coming from. And strangely, no one considered the chair as the source.

IF YOUR CURRENT JOB SUCKS, THE BEST THING YOU CAN DO FOR YOURSELF IS TO GO FORTH AND FLOURISH ELSEWHERE.

I do like to think that Karma takes care of revenge for us (and I probably deserve a whack with a self-help book for that one, too), but my mother always told me that success is the best revenge. This means if your current job sucks, the best thing you can do for yourself is to go forth and flourish elsewhere. My friend's revenge story is a good one, and I know it came from stifling rage over four years of abuse, but I wouldn't recommend it. It all comes back around.

Revenge

5. Have a plan before you quit. Ideally you'll have another job all lined up. It is possible to seek employment while you are gainfully employed; you just have to be careful about how you handle it.

PLANNING YOUR ESCAPE

* Don't use your current work e-mail to communicate with potential new employers. Use your personal e-mail, as long as your personal e-mail isn't something tacky like hottgirl92@whatever.com or hardcoregirl@biteme.net. If it is, do yourself and your potential future boss a favor and get a grown-up e-mail address.

* Don't post your résumé on job-seeker Web sites. You can search jobs (on your home computer—not the one at work) and apply for them without having to post your résumé.

* Don't discuss your job search with coworkers, even if you consider them to be friends. Once you've found a new job, you can tell them first, and it will make them feel better about your not confiding in them sooner. Again, trust no one!

* When scheduling interviews, don't lie to your current employer. Simply request a personal day (if you have earned time off), or try to schedule it first thing in the morning or late in the afternoon and tell your boss you have an appointment. It's not a lie if you don't say with whom.

* When interviewing, be upfront with your potential new employer and tell them that your boss is unaware that you're "exploring your options." Let them know they can contact all the other references you've supplied on your résumé, but that your current employer might react negatively to your "option exploring."

✳ Never disparage your current boss to a potential employer. I've conducted hundreds of interviews, and this is a deal killer. If I interview someone who tells me how awful her boss is (even if he is awful), I always imagine her having the same discussion with someone else about me down the road. And by the way, just because you think your boss is an ass doesn't mean the next person he hires will.

✳ Use your current job as a mental checklist to evaluate your next. Arm yourself for interviews with a list of questions so that, at the least, you can make sure you're not walking into same situation in a different building.

6. Take no prisoners. You may have friends/coworkers tell you, "If you leave I will too." Strongly discourage them. This is very bad form and leaves you with little bargaining room. **Never incite a mass walkout.** If they choose to leave later, it's their responsibility and not yours.

7. Put yourself in your boss's shoes. How would you like an employee on your team to break the news that she's moving on? Be gentle, be kind, but be firm. Entertain counteroffers, but never disclose the hand you're holding (i.e., never tell your current employer what your new salary will be—but feel free to tell him it's more in line with what your skills are worth).

8. Don't make it more painful than it has to be. The general rule is two weeks' notice. I've given more in the past and regretted it. No matter what you do, it will be a miserable two weeks. Do you really want to drag it out for a month or more out of a misguided sense of loyalty?

FINDING COMPANY RIGHT

I've always thought that interviewing for a new job is like dating. You put your best outfit on and your best foot forward, and you try to show off your best side. Sometimes there's instant attraction. Sometimes you have to work a little harder. But, also like dating, it's really important to hide your desperation. You could be their dream employee, but if you come off desperate, they're either going to lose your résumé, or lowball you on a starting salary. These are the key things to remember in an interview:

❋ **You're not looking for a job.** You're "investigating your options."

❋ **You want them to like you more than you like them** (or at least, make it appear that way).

❋ **Never act like you *need* the job.** They need *you*.

❋ **Be prepared**—research the company beforehand and drop a few comments here and there to show that you've done the legwork ("I really admire the acquisition you pulled off last year; I'll bet that was great for your bottom line"). Flattery does work, in dating and in business, but try not to sound like you're ass kissing. Your compliments and comments should be sincere.

❋ **Before your date, I mean interview, take some time to think about how your skills and talent can contribute to Company Right.** Whether they ask during the interview or not, it will help you assess if Company Right is indeed the right company for you.

❋ **You don't have to fall in love with the company immediately,** but do allow them to sell themselves. Ask questions about benefits, frequency of performance reviews and raises, perks, and so on. If it seems a little cold and calculating, it's because it is. That's the business world, and if you want to make more money, you have to start establishing your expectations on the first date.

* **Be willing to turn it down.** Your interview went well, you think the job might be for you, but the salary is not only less than what you're making now, it's also lower than industry average (because I know you looked it up on Salary.com first, right?). No matter how poor the job market, you have to be willing and able to tell Company Right that they just offered you a Salary Wrong. The nicest way to do this (and the easiest, because nice really shouldn't matter here anyway) is to simply say, "I appreciate the offer and I would certainly love to commit, but I was thinking more along the lines of $[ballpark figure]. *Is there any room to negotiate?*" And then be very, very quiet. Say no more. Offer no more concessions. Don't tell them you'll meet them in the middle. *Wait* and see what they come up with next. If it isn't a counteroffer (or an offer to call you back after they find out if there is any wiggle room), then thank them kindly and move on to the next company. Accepting a job with a company that isn't willing to compensate you according to industry standards is a bad idea, and I see it as a warning that there will be more trouble down the road (kind of like that guy you went on a date with last year who got up to use the restroom as soon as the check arrived).

> **READY TO QUIT IN A FIT, BUT DON'T WANT TO BURN YOUR BRIDGES?** VISIT *WWW.IQUIT.ORG* FOR ADVICE, ETIQUETTE—EVEN SAMPLE RESIGNATION LETTERS—THAT ENSURE YOU'LL MAKE A GRACEFUL EXIT.

CHAPTER ELEVEN

STICKING IT OUT

Let's say you've made every mistake in the book (or, in this book, every mistake in Chapter 6: Damage Control: You Break It, You Fix It), but you've decided to give it one more try instead of moving on.

Is it fixable?

Unless you were embezzling from the company (or doing anything else illegal), nothing is beyond repair. Or, on the other hand, your job makes you so miserable that you're ready to pretty up your résumé and start hitting the streets in search for a new one.

Does that mean that you can't make it work in the job that you already have? Not necessarily.

Consider your current Job O'Misery: Your boss is a demon, your coworkers are harpies, your paycheck is so tiny that you're thinking about selling your blood so you can buy groceries, and you spend most days dreaming about what it would be like somewhere else. The question you have to ask yourself is: *Is it the job, or is it ME?*

I hate to put this out there, sweetie, but it just might be you. Is your boss a demon because she insists that you show up to work on time? Yes, you're a free spirit and clocks have never been your thing, but consider for just a moment that you boss might be a perfectly reasonable person who simply wants her employees to be at work at the designated start time. Or are you feeling that your coworkers are mean, vicious, and you can't trust them as far as you can throw them? Here's another wake-up call (just like the ones you should have been scheduling to get your tail to the office on time): Your coworkers are not your friends.

THE MORE INCOMPETENT YOUR BOSS IS ON THIS JOB, THE BETTER EVERY OTHER BOSS YOU HAVE IN YOUR LIFE WILL SEEM.

The business world isn't like summer camp. You cannot expect any of the following from a job in the real world: Bonding. Loyalty. Friendship. Braiding each others' hair. Sitting around a campfire singing "Cumbaya." I'm not saying that you can't make friends at work. What I *am* saying is that if your expectations from a job are similar to the expectations you had for your sorority, you're going to be sorely disappointed. If there is disharmony in the ranks and it seems to be directed at you, it's because the wolves can sense weakness and they're circling. Backbiting from coworkers sucks, but it's a given on almost any job where employees compete for attention, titles, accounts, and raises. It's not just your job—it's every job.

When I left my job at a software company to freelance, I assumed I'd also be leaving the bitching, backstabbing, attention-grabbing, and infighting behind. Instead, I found the exact same thing, except this time I was the new girl and competing in a larger arena with more experienced wolves than I. I worked for editors who seemed to enjoy sending back copy for rewrite after rewrite, publishers I had to practically threaten to sue before they'd send me a measly $200 check for four days of work, assistant editors who changed three words in my piece and replaced my byline with theirs, and other writers who stole assignments right out from under me. Did I cry about it? No. The fact that I had to deal with the same crazy behavior that made me run screaming from my corporate job was an unpleasant revelation, but I wanted to do this writing thing badly enough that I was willing to put up with it. What did surprise me is how well six years in a job that I hated prepared me to deal with the mean girls of the publishing world.

So how do you turn a "bad job" into a good one without heading for the hills? **Perspective.** Instead of seeing your job as a soul-sucking maze of lost opportunities and corporate pep rallies, why not look at it like a boot camp for the future? The more incompetent your boss is on this job, the better every

THE MORE DIFFICULT YOUR COWORKERS ARE NOW, THE MORE YOU'LL BE HAPPILY SURPRISED WHEN YOU FINALLY DO FIND YOURSELF IN A POSITION WHERE YOU'RE ACTUALLY PART OF A COLLABORATIVE TEAM.

other boss you have in your life will seem. The more difficult your coworkers are now, the more you'll be happily surprised when you finally do find yourself in a position where you're actually part of a collaborative team.

I don't want to scare you, but suppose you do leave your job-from-hell and discover that the shiny new job is just a Twilight Zone, alternate universe version of your old job? What then? If working for yourself is not an option, the perspective you need right now is an understanding of how things work in the corporate world—and that's *any* job in the corporate world, not just yours.

Cash is king. Money is the bottom line and if you're not contributing, you're going to be treated like a second-class citizen. Grumbling about what's "fair" (or not fair) isn't going to take you very far. Sometimes you have to suck it up, jump on the bandwagon, and do what it takes to keep the company in the black—even if it means working a lot for a little in hopes of a payoff down the line. In most cases, the payoff *will* come. And if it doesn't, remember that the door is always open.

Reality bites. And it doesn't apologize. If you're expecting your boss to be a substitute parent, friend, confidante, or shrink, you're setting yourself up to fail. Your boss will shine the light of happiness on you as long as you're outperforming the rest of the crew. Fall behind, and you're going to be in the dark. If you can't deal with the ups and downs, the corporate world is going to eat you alive and you'd be better off farming a small parcel of land in West Virginia.

Your best can always be better. Even if you are the golden girl, don't expect to rest on your laurels for very long. The better you are, the more you'll be expected to do. The farther you pull ahead of the pack, the harder you're going to have to work to stay ahead. It's a long drop from arrogance to humility. You'll be safer (and saner) if you accept accolades and understand that expectations will be higher. If you find yourself resenting your boss for expecting more from you than your coworkers, just remember that it means you're doing something right. No one likes (or promotes) a martyr.

EVEN IF YOU ARE THE GOLDEN GIRL, DON'T EXPECT TO REST ON YOUR LAURELS FOR VERY LONG.

Life is not fair. Oh, how it used to piss me off when my mother said that to me. But in retrospect, it prepared me for the injustices of the working world. At some point in your career, someone is going to get promoted over you and they won't deserve it. Someone who isn't as smart as you are is going to make more money than you do and it won't be fair. This is not license for you to say, "To hell with it—I'm going to do the minimum to get by just like everyone else."

Working hard does pay off; sometimes just not right away. But that person who got promoted over you is going to end up in over her head. The one who seems incapable of changing a lightbulb, yet earns twice your salary, will eventually become one of your boss's mistakes. And you'll be right there, standing by, ready to pick up the pieces.

TURNING IT AROUND

Creating a brand new you just might change your bad old job into the job of your dreams. There are steps you can take—no matter what mistakes have been made or how discouraged you've become—to turn your work situation into one that you love. No matter what your job, it always starts with Y-O-U.

1. Make a list. Make several lists if you have to. The first one should be your goals for the next twelve months. Fill in point A, where you are now, and point Z, where you want to be, and then fill in everything in between. If you're currently in an entry level job, have made several fruitless attempts to advance, and feel like you're stuck, all you have to do is something different than what you've been doing. If you keep making the same mistakes, you're going to get the same results. Maybe it's just a different approach, a lateral move in the same company, or simply taking a different tack in dealing with your direct supervisor. Everything goes on the list.

2. Understand that it takes time. You can't change how others perceive you overnight, or just by showing up for work on time for a few weeks. If your work ethic (or lack thereof) has been holding you back on the job, expect to work twice as hard for twice as long to make a comeback. If you expect immediate fanfare and flowers and balloons because you've suddenly

167

STICKING IT OUT

TO **HUMILITY**

become a model employee, you're going to be disappointed. But if you have a plan to apply intensive effort over a long period of time, if it happens sooner you'll be pleasantly surprised.

3. Don't try to do it on your own. Enlist the help of a (trusted!) friend or colleague— preferably someone you don't work with directly—to go over your twelve-month plan. Ask this person to speak frankly about areas she feels you could improve (and don't make excuses when she does, otherwise she'll clam up). Accept the generous criticism, don't take it personally (you asked for it!), and take lots of notes. If there are flaws you're already aware of, see if this person has advice on how you can be better. For example, I realize I have a tendency to be arrogant and that my arrogance can come across as condescension. It's something I have to consciously work on. I'm lucky enough to have a boss who feels comfortable giving me a signal when I "go there"—and I don't make her feel bad when she does it. In fact, I thank her for helping me grow as a person. Humility goes a long way in the workplace and you can't fake it. It helps that I have honest people around to take me down a peg or

if you keep making the **same mistakes**................

two when necessary. If you allow hurt feelings to show every time someone offers criticism, you're going to end up isolated and it will slow your professional growth.

4. Don't take everything so seriously. You have to be able to laugh at yourself, and at your situation. I work for a large corporation that speaks corporation-ese. Do I get annoyed when I have to attend a meta-meeting (a meeting about a meeting)? Yes, but I also think it's funny. Do some corporate policies make me want to stick a fork in my eye? Yes, but I also think they're funny. We have forms for performance reviews that are standard and not meant for what you might call "creatives." There is a section on the form about safety in the office, particularly around hazardous machinery. I could just write "N/A" in that section, but hating to leave a blank, I amuse myself and get creative. One year I wrote: *Kelly never runs with scissors.* Another: *No one has been fatally injured by the postage machine in forty-seven months.* If the company you work for sometimes makes you feel like you've been plopped down in the middle of a living and breathing Dilbert cartoon, try laughing about it instead of bitching. Trust me, almost everyone else is laughing with you. Except for Human Resources. They don't think you're funny, either.

5. Your job is not your life. The biggest mistake I've ever made on any job (including drinking too much at the holiday party, crying, having tantrums, dating coworkers, etc.) was letting a job take over my life. I blamed the job, but I should have

. . . . .you're going to get the same results

blamed myself. I was so wrapped up in my job that everything else—friends, family, social life—fell by the wayside. When I finally woke up and realized that the job was all I had left, I also realized that the job wasn't all that great to begin with. And that was the beginning of the worst emotional period in my life, to date. It took me many months to rebuild the support and connections in my personal life. When I began channeling less energy into the job and more into my private life, what

META-MEETING

STICKING IT OUT

surprised me is that my work didn't suffer. The office didn't fall apart without me, I was still doing quite well and handling everything I did before, plus I was happier because the job no longer consumed every aspect of my life. When it got rough at work, I had something else going on to distract me. I had people I could call, friends I could see, and wine I could drink at happy hour with non-work-related associates. It took a lot of effort to turn it around, but it made me realize that no job is worth sacrificing my mental health. If I can be just as good for forty-hours-a-week as I was at sixty-hours-a-week, what kind of idiot would I be if I persisted at putting in the extra time? A friendless one, that's what kind. Even if you have to make a little sign to hang above your computer screen: **It's Just a Job,** or something else that reminds you not to get too entangled in the thing that you do to pay your bills, do it. Be open with your friends and ask them to tell you when you're blowing them off too often for work. It's easier for me now, but even years later, I still need the reminders and reality checks.

6. Schedule a sit down. This is a new beginning for you and you know it, but your boss should know it, too. It's not going to be easy—and it can be touchy—but if you're going to turn things around you need your boss on your side. Let's say you had the performance review that made you want to quit a month ago. You've been seething ever since. But now you're reading this and wondering if there was something else you could have done. There is. You can do now what you should have done during your negative review: Enlist your boss's help in coming up with an action plan to turn the negatives into positives. Sure, you sat there for an hour feeling like you were being pecked by hungry ducks, hearing your work torn apart, your ideas shot down, your work ethic criticized. But did you hear anything but the negative? Did you ask for help? More training? Did you come up with a plan to be better at what you do? If not, you can't blame the company or your boss. It's not too late.

Schedule a "post-review" meeting with your boss and approach the subject calmly and rationally. What are your options for additional training? Will your boss accept an addendum to your review that includes target goals for the next year? Is there anything specific your boss expects from you that didn't come up during your review? Make sure she understands you want to turn this around, that you want to keep your job, and that you are passionate about your career. Most bosses will be receptive to this brand of honesty and more than willing to help you come up with a plan to make your next review a positive one.

ENLIST YOUR BOSS'S HELP IN COMING UP WITH AN ACTION PLAN TO TURN THE NEGATIVES INTO POSITIVES.

7. Live your list. Once you have something put together—a list of goals, areas for improvement, a game plan, additional training, etc.—make it part of your life. Incorporate the goals into your online calendar and set up weekly reminders for specific tasks so you won't forget where you're headed. Having smaller items ("Learn HTML and CSS" or "Customer Service Training") to check off is a great motivator. If you don't use an online calendar, print your list and make it part of your day planner. Break your goals down into manageable tasks and distribute them throughout your dated book. Make a note of all achievements and milestones (you'll need these later when your next performance review rolls around).

t a job…it's just a job…it's just a job…it's just a job…it's just a

THE WAITING GAME

I once read a statistic that one negative employee can impact the behavior of seven people in the same office. In other words, one whiner can turn a small staff into a pack of whiners. Let's assume you're not the office Little Miss Negative (and I hope you're not), but her bad juju is bringing everyone else down. You've talked to your boss, who doesn't seem in a hurry to do anything about it. You've reached your breaking point. If Little Miss Negative isn't out in a hurry, what else can you do but start looking somewhere else? *Don't do it. She's not worth it.* And, chances are, your boss is more clued in to the problem child in the office than you think she is. Even if that isn't the case, these things have a way of working themselves out.

> ONE WHINER CAN TURN A SMALL STAFF INTO A PACK OF WHINERS.

Several years ago, I worked with a fairly small staff (that shall remain nameless) that also included a Little Miss Negative (who also shall remain nameless). Though I hired this person, I was not aware of her negative . . . let's call them "personality traits" . . . until she'd been on the job for a few months. After complaints from several other staff members ("She's greedy," "She's a whiner," "She stole my idea") and personally witnessing several of these behaviors during staff meetings, I had a talk with Miss Negative. She immediately burst into tears, unleashed a litany of complaints about other employees that must have been damming up for weeks, and basically blamed everyone else for her bad behavior. The meeting itself was surreal—like trying to convince a five-year-old that biting the other children is wrong when the five-year-old

> PERSONALITY TRAITS

is positive that everyone else deserves a good bite. In fact, before leaving my office, she literally stamped her foot mid-tantrum. After things cooled down, I spoke to her again and suggested that she might fit in better elsewhere. I didn't fire her; I just gave her the opportunity to look for another job with my blessing. When she found one, my team was overjoyed, and frankly I was relieved that she would soon be someone else's problem.

Unfortunately, working in a small industry in a mid-sized city, I should have known that I was just shuffling her off on another set of employees—some with whom I was acquainted. In just a few weeks on her new job she was up to her old tricks, something I discovered when a friend who now worked with my former problem employee called to ask, "Whyyyyyyy?" Why didn't I warn them? Why did I foist her off on them?

First, her new employer never called me to check references. In fact, the new employer thought she was pulling a fast one and snagging one of my best employees out from under me (poaching employees isn't illegal, but it is definitely frowned upon if one wishes to have collegial relationships with others in the same industry). If the new employer had called and asked the right questions, I would have been fair but honest about some of the problems my former employee created for our staff. Because she didn't, they were stuck with her. Even when I got an e-mail: "Are you mad at me for offering Little Miss Negative the job?" I responded with a friendly, "Not at all—I'm sure she'll be a good fit." And I genuinely hoped she would be.

But some months later, I had lunch with a colleague who now had to share an office with our former Little Miss Negative. "She steals everyone's ideas," said my friend. "She

Whyyyyyy?

1

NOTHING LASTS
FOREVER.
GIVE IT ENOUGH TIME
AND YOU'LL FIND
THAT **THINGS WORK
THEMSELVES OUT.**

2

WAITING OFTEN PAYS
OFF.

whines and cries until she gets her way. She's like a child!" I felt terrible, because I knew what she was going through, but the only advice I could give her was to let out enough rope and let Little Miss Negative tie herself in knots with it until her new boss realized how damaging her behavior was for the staff. Unfortunately, it took a few loyal staffers jumping ship and another year before the new boss woke up and made Little Miss Negative walk the plank, but my friend was glad she waited it out. Not only did she weather the storm, but she also proved to her boss that she could handle working with the most difficult personality—and do so with grace. She complained only when it was justified and when proof was in hand. She didn't bitch about Little Miss Negative's behavior to other coworkers. In fact, she made an attempt to befriend Little Miss Negative and try to help her modify her foot-stamping, temper-tantrum-having, power-pouting behavior. After almost two years of babysitting, biting her tongue, and having to endure a number of indignities, my friend organized Little Miss Negative's going away party. A few months later, she was offered her boss's job.

There are two lessons to be learned here: One, nothing lasts forever. Give it enough time and you'll find that things work themselves out. And two, waiting often pays off. You don't have to be manipulative; you just have to be stubborn. The job you hate today very well might be the job of your dreams tomorrow, once everything shakes out the right way. Stick-to-itiveness has its perks.

IT'S NOT YOU, IT'S THEM

What if it really isn't you? Ask anyone working in the corporate world for any length of time if they've ever suffered due to inept management, clueless supervisors, or incompetent bosses and you'll likely hear countless stories of all of the above. If you're thinking about leaving a job because you don't like (or agree with, or respect) your boss, consider this: Every mid-to-large-sized organization has its share of bad employees. One of those could be your boss. One of them could be your boss on the next job you apply for. And the next. If you leave every job that isn't exactly ideal, you're going to do a lot of job hopping. The key to making the job you have now the one that works for you is learning how to manage your boss.

THE KEY TO MAKING THE JOB YOU HAVE NOW THE ONE THAT WORKS FOR YOU IS LEARNING HOW TO MANAGE YOUR BOSS.

She's unreasonable, irrational, and has ludicrous expectations. One day, she'll ask you for notes on Project A by first thing in the morning.

JOB HOPPING

After you work into the wee hours putting everything together, she'll tell you to forget it—now she needs notes on another project entirely. Do you pull your hair out, scream, and start working on your résumé? If it makes you feel better. But if you want to stick with it, you're going to have to suck it up and deliver. Instead of fuming and resenting your boss, why not just assume that something transpired behind the scenes that you're not aware of—things shift quickly in the business world—and move on to the next assignment.

When I was freelancing, I often accepted assignments from one editor that would end up in the lap of a different editor weeks later. I'd complete the original assignment, then receive notes back for a rewrite on what would essentially

What can I do?

be a completely different piece. Did it matter to the new editor that the first gave me a specific assignment and I did what was asked? Not at all. Did I snarl about it privately? Definitely. Did I complain to the editor's boss? Absolutely not—that's a no-no in my business. Did I still want to get a check for the assignment? Yes, so I did the rewrite, no questions asked. Because I'd worked in the corporate world for a boss who wasn't always clear with her direction, who shifted task so often it was difficult to keep up on a daily basis, and who didn't think morale was something she had to worry about, working with bipolar editors was a breeze.

I've heard nightmare stories from other friends in the freelance world who worked for the same editors I did—ranting phone calls late at night, nasty e-mails, dropped assignments, and various other indignities. One writer friend, upon being given a different direction for her article, e-mailed the editor's boss with her finished product and the editor's original notes for the assignment. Not only did she piss the editor off, but she also blew any chance of writing for them again by going over the editor's head. Publishers and executive editors almost always stand behind their editor—not the freelancer. My friend's piece was dropped and she wasn't asked to write for the publication again.

Sucking it up when you feel like exploding isn't fun, but sometimes it's what you have to do to pay your dues in the world of business. I have another friend who started her career in the world of nonprofits. She wanted to make a difference and work on something that she really cared about, and was willing to take a lower-paying entry level job in order to do that. Initially, everything was perfect. Her boss was warm and kind, the executive director was passionate about the cause, and her coworkers were part of a hard-working team. But in just a few months, my friend realized that her boss's demeanor was a cover for a definitive lack of experience and management skills. Her coworkers' strong bond was akin to the bond hostages develop in survival situations. The executive director, while a strong advocate for the cause, was a board member for several organizations and a social calendar that seldom left room for the nonprofit my friend worked for. After just three months on the job, she was ready to quit—just like four or five of her counterparts that came before her. It was only her second job out of college and she was concerned about how it would look on her résumé, leaving a job after only three months.

SUCKING IT UP WHEN YOU FEEL LIKE EXPLODING ISN'T FUN, BUT SOMETIMES IT'S WHAT YOU HAVE TO DO.

She spent another couple of months on the fence, partially hoping her job would be cut and that the problem would be solved for her.

When we spoke about it, I asked her what she had done to change the situation. "What can I do?" she asked. "I'm not in charge there." From what she'd told me, it didn't sound like anyone was in charge or accountable. "What if you were in charge?" I asked. "What would you do?" She rattled off a list, starting with ways to improve staff morale and ending with a specific idea for a volunteer

What if you were in charge?

program. "Have you pitched these ideas to anyone?" I asked. "Why should I? It wouldn't do any good." She was so discouraged that her dream job had turned into a nightmare almost overnight that she was ready to just give up and walk away. I told her to give it a shot. It wouldn't kill her career to try talking to the executive director about her ideas, plus if she was ready to walk away anyway, what did she have to lose?

My friend ended up putting her ideas together and pitching them over lunch to her executive director. She discovered that the director was more than receptive, surprised to learn that morale was low (since she depended on my friend's boss to handle such things), and that she absolutely loved my friend's ideas. In fact, within six months, my friend was offered her boss's job working directly for the executive director and is now running a very successful nonprofit organization—and she's not even thirty yet.

PEOPLE OFTEN LEAVE
bad jobs
not because of the job itself,
BUT BECAUSE OF
A BAD BOSS.

That's one way to deal with a bad management situation and my friend is glad she stuck it out. In my experience, people often leave bad jobs not because of the job itself, but because of a bad boss. It doesn't have to be that way if you can learn how to manage upward.

1. Throw out the labels. One key mistake is to label your boss "bad," which implies a hopeless situation. At best, you can manage your boss into a level of competency that you can work with. At the worst, you can change your own behavior so that your boss's lack of management skills won't impact your day-to-day workload.

> AT BEST, YOU CAN MANAGE YOUR BOSS INTO A LEVEL OF COMPETENCY THAT YOU CAN WORK WITH.

2. Understand your boss's motivation. Does she become defensive when questioned? Perhaps she's more aware of her shortcomings than you thought. Many people get defensive when they're trying to hide their own lack of competency. Instead of cornering your boss, try to isolate what the problem is and offer to be part of the solution. If she has difficulty managing your team, why not discuss her appointing a "team lead" to be responsible for the staff's requests? That way, she only has to deal with one person (hopefully you) and you get to manage the team. Problem solved.

> AT THE WORST, YOU CAN CHANGE YOUR OWN BEHAVIOR SO THAT YOUR BOSS'S LACK OF MANAGEMENT SKILLS WON'T IMPACT YOUR DAY-TO-DAY WORKLOAD.

3. Have some empathy. Do you really know what your boss has to deal with on a day-to-day basis? It seems like she turns a deaf ear to your requests, but is she getting requests from all sides? If she's middle management, she has a boss to report to as well. Putting yourself in her shoes will help you better understand why she's not perfect in every way.

4. Stop complaining. And if you can, stop your coworkers from doing the same. You'll win a lot of points (both from your boss and for your future career) if you can help everyone on your staff change their perspective. Sure, there's a lot to complain about. But it's not going to get you anywhere and it takes a lot of energy you could be using to formulate a positive plan.

5. Be grateful for your boss's shortcomings. Her faults mean that there are places where you can step up. See them as an opportunity for you instead of the bane of your existence. After all, if your boss was perfect, how would you ever fill her shoes?

> AFTER ALL, IF YOUR BOSS WAS PERFECT, HOW WOULD YOU EVER FILL HER SHOES?

6. Make your own decisions. If your boss is indecisive, you are going to have to be the decisive one. Sometimes it's a simple matter of insecurity on your boss's part. If you ask and get the usual "non answer," move forward and deal with the consequences later. At least something will get done and chances are good that your hesitant boss will appreciate your willingness to take the risk.

7. Stand your ground. If your boss is a bully, she'll never respect someone who backs down. This doesn't mean you have to be bully number two—pushing back rarely works. But being firm is something that a bully respects, and it helps set up boundaries for how far you're willing to be pushed.

8. Take the initiative. If your boss is a poor communicator, you're in the perfect position to take on that role. Again, see if it's just a matter of her being overworked. Can you step in and help? Can you be the person who makes sure everyone knows what they're supposed to know? If you handle this with tact, your boss won't see it as an affront; she'll be grateful for the assistance (and you can add it to your list of achievements for your next performance review). Don't wait to get what you need. Initiate the meeting, conversation, or project on your own.

9. Be on her side. No matter how irrational, incompetent, or indecisive your boss, as her employee your job is to be on her team. It doesn't mean you have to agree with her work style; you just have to work with her. If personality is the issue, it's unlikely she's going to change just because you don't like who she is. But you can change how you respond to certain behaviors. Does she call you late at night? Tell her you have a new policy to manage your work stress and it starts with not answering your phone after six o'clock. Does she have temper tantrums? Leave the area until she calms down and let her come to you when she is. If you make it clear that you're both working toward the same goal (your individual career advancement as well as the company's success) you can be a team instead of sworn enemies.

Your **boss's boss** *probably*
DOESN'T WANT TO HEAR THAT YOU'RE HAVING A
PERSONALITY
CONFLICT

10. Only go over her head if you're willing to walk. In most organizations, complaining about your boss to her boss is basically the same thing as signing your own pink slip. Your boss's boss probably doesn't want to hear that you're having a personality conflict, plus it backs the person in charge into a corner. What result are you looking for? Do you want her to talk to your boss? Put her on probation? Fire her? It's going to come back to spite you. That doesn't mean that it's impossible. Like my friend who works for the nonprofit organization, bringing a solution to the table rather than a litany of problems actually worked in her favor. She wasn't complaining; she was offering a list of ideas to make the organization more profitable and a happier place to work. Rather than backing the director into a corner where she'd have to act (fire the manager, or my friend), she gave her the opportunity to work with her to resolve the problems everyone had been complaining about.

There are a few rare instances of unmanageable (or abusive) bosses that are beyond fixing. In those cases, don't put yourself in a position where you're stuck working for someone who has questionable ethics or anger management problems. No job is worth that. But these scenarios are few and far between. It's more likely that changing your workplace is simply a matter of changing your perspective and your reaction to specific behavior. And if you do it right, your boss will never even know that you're "managing up." Learning how to navigate the politics of the business world takes time. Be patient, stick it out, and you just might find that your Job O'Misery has become the job of your dreams.

CHECKPOINTS FOR A HIGHER PAYCHECK

Hold it!

Before you start paving your career path full force or shattering the bejesus out of that glass ceiling it's time to recap the valuable lessons you've learned.

While some of us are obsessed with creating lists on a daily basis, undoubtedly everyone loves being able to save a little time. In the following pages you'll find quick and quirky checklists to help put your current situation into perspective. You'll be able to track where you stand now at your job and, more importantly, focus your attention on where you want to be (at the top, girl).

Take a deep breath, take the cap off your lucky ballpoint pen, and start taking notes. I've given you all the tools you need to get ahead.

Now it's time to put 'em to work!

SUREFIRE CAREER KILLERS ... OR HOW TO LOSE A PROMOTION IN 10 DAYS

If you're into chick flicks then you've probably already seen Kate Hudson and Matthew McConaughey star in the 2003 romantic comedy, *How to Lose a Guy in 10 Days*. Hudson's character, women's magazine writer Andie Anderson, is assigned to come up with a creative article on how to get rid of a guy in less than two weeks. If she's able to pull the questionable stunt off, she'll be rewarded with the freedom to write about the stuff that really matters to her. Does the new promotion you were just handed really matter to you? If so, read on to make sure it stays yours. Most companies embrace change and you don't want your new, higher salary changing for the worse!

☑ **1. Call in sick with "female problems."**
   Surely, your boss is just dying to know that you (a) have cramps and (b) that they're bad enough that you can't drive your car or sit in front of a computer. Come on, ladies. The days of writhing in pain and lying in bed with a hot water bottle on your abdomen once a month are long over. That's why God made Tylenol.®

☑ **2. Gossip.**
   Gossiping about coworkers will earn you the reputation of being someone who revels in the misfortune of others. Even if you're only dishing about celebrities, you'll still get a reputation as someone who isn't professional.

☑ **3. Have "personality conflicts" with coworkers.**

It takes two to tango, and even the most difficult person to get along with requires your participation in order to create a conflict.

☑ **4. Cultivate a sense of entitlement.**

Sure, you're great at your job, and you definitely deserve more money for doing it. But if you expect a lot for a little, like a promotion after only six months on the job, you're going to be disappointed.

☑ **5. Keep your head down and your mouth shut.**

There are people like this in every workplace—they just want to keep the job and paycheck they have. They don't want to stir the pot. These people don't get promoted. The ones who are innovative, inquisitive, and willing to throw ideas out during a meeting like it's a skeet-shooting competition are the ones who advance in their careers. *They take initiative and they get noticed.*

☑ **6. Be resistant to change.**

Groan in meetings when you hear the company is implementing new software. Make snide remarks when the CEO sends out restructuring e-mails. Scoff at the company head's plan for expansion. Then watch while your coworkers who jump on board set sail—without you.

☑ **7. Show up late.**

Even if you have a creative job in a flexible work environment, being on time sets a good example for other people and it shows your boss that you care. Become a habitual latecomer and you might as well add "flaky" to your job description.

☑ **8. Fear higher-ups.**

Some people steer clear of corporate VIPs because they're afraid of saying or doing the wrong things. If you want to get ahead, you have to do the exact opposite. Think about it: You can't get promoted if the CEO doesn't even know you exist.

☑ **9. Respond negatively to criticism.**

Instead of looking at every critique as a "teaching moment," allow your anger or hurt feelings to override your motivation to become a better whatever. If your boss stops offering feedback, it's time to start worrying (and probably start looking for another job).

☑ **10. Be timid.**

If you seem hesitant or apprehensive when assigned more responsibility or a larger project than what you're used to tackling, you probably won't ever get offered much more.

CHECKPOINTS FOR A HIGHER PAYCHECK

KEEPING YOUR EYES ON THE PRIZE
... OR HER CORNER OFFICE

The old cliché is that honesty is always the best policy. In the case of coveting your boss's job, that is indeed the way to go. However, there are a few words that immediately come to mind—think: *direct*, but *delicate* and *discreet*—and you should probably learn the meanings of them before you march on over to her office and start a knockin'. Read on, Motivated Mama, read on.

 1. Speak up.

Make sure your boss is aware that you're interested in—at some point, down the road, in the far future—being promoted into her job so that she can be promoted to the next rung. Don't do this during the job interview, on your first day at work, or via an intermediary (i.e., don't tell anyone else *but* your boss). The best time to express interest in being her right-hand woman and next in line for her job would be during your first (or second, or third, or any) performance review.

 2. Be encouraging.

A good boss with an eye on moving up the ladder will hire employees she can groom to take over her job responsibilities. We can't get promoted until there's someone next in line. However, your boss may not be as astute as some and might require some encouragement.

☑ 3. **Be tactful.**

Rather than simply stating, "I want your job," or asking, "How can I get your job?" a more tactful approach would be: "How can I help *you* move up in the company?" Pay attention when your boss gets new assignments, offer to help lighten her workload, find out if there's anything she'd be willing to delegate to you. The best employee acts as support staff for her boss—and often gets promoted as a result.

☑ 4. **Be considerate.**

Make sure your boss understands that you don't want her out of her chair so you can hop in while the seat's still warm. You have to find out what her work goals are. Maybe she doesn't want to be CEO someday. In that case, just keep doing what you're doing and be nice about it—she might be working for you in a few years and you don't want to burn any bridges.

☑ 5. **Know her job.**

It sounds simple, but do you really know what your boss's job responsibilities are? Do you know what she does on a day-to-day basis? If so, make sure you really want her job before you start gunning for it. Ideally you should try to learn everything about it, inside and out.

☑ 6. **Check in regularly.**

Is there anything you can do to make her job easier? Are you doing everything you possibly can to make sure she doesn't have to go behind you? Does she trust your work? If the answer is anything but a resounding "yes!" you still have work to do in your own job before you start training for hers.

☑ 7. **Pay attention to your boss and allow her to lead you.**
Is she in the office every day until 6 p.m.? You should
be right there with her. Does she grumble about having too much on her plate? Ask if you can help (and
mean it).

☑ 8. **Be a team player.**
You and your boss should work together to advance
her career. Why? Because in most cases you can't get
promoted unless she does.

☑ 9. **Be her champion.**
Managing staff is difficult, particularly if you're in a
middle management situation where you're responsible both for your own success and the success of
the employees on your team. Whenever possible, you
should make sure your boss's boss is aware of her
successes. Even if it's just a "Hey, did you hear about
my boss landing that account?" in passing in the hall-
way to the company CEO, it shows that you're not
only supporting your boss, but that you're also
invested in her success.

☑ 10. **Be grateful.**
The old adage, "never bite the hand that feeds you,"
couldn't be more appropriate when we're talking
about moving up the corporate ladder. Become
power-hungry (or even power-fixated) once you're
promoted, and you're going to make enemies. If your
boss helps you climb a rung or two, don't make the
mistake of assuming you could have done it on your
own. You never know when it might come back to
bite you in the end.

SHOW ME THE MONEY
. . . OR WAIT A BIT

You love your current job—really, you do—but you still aren't making enough money to quit that second job just yet or resorting to Ramen Noodles right before that two-week pay period mark is starting to make you consider eating Fluffy or Fido. What's a struggling girl to do? The easiest, most direct answer is this: *Ask for a raise*. Oh, it sounds so simple—but just a sec. Before you schedule a meeting with the Head Honcho, make sure you know exactly what you want, and more importantly, exactly what you're *worth*. Here are ten reasons to hold off on holding out your paw for a fatter paycheck.

☑ 1. **The company is undergoing restructuring and lay-offs are a possibility.**

   Even if you've been assured that your job is safe, wait until the smoke clears before you ask for an increase in salary. If job cuts are going on behind the scenes, hitting your boss up for a raise tells your boss two things: First, you're going to be expensive. Second, you don't understand your own company's financial situation well enough to know that it's a bad time to put the impetus on your boss to come up with money in the budget for your raise while she's trying to figure out how not to lay off other key staff members.

☑ 2. **If you've recently been admonished for underperforming, taking too much sick time, being late, having conflicts with other employees, or otherwise not living up to the expectations of your job.**

> > > > > > >

Hopefully, none of this will be the case, but you should be aware that these things live in your employee file (and your boss's brain) for longer than they stick with you. I have a six-month rule with employees—if they've been told there's a problem with their performance, I give them six months to correct it. If it doesn't happen again in a six-month period, I wipe the slate clean.

☑ 3. **When it's not on the schedule.**

In the corporate world, many companies have mid-year or annual reviews. If you're asking for a raise outside of the performance review schedule, you'd better have a good reason (like taking on new and higher level responsibilities—but make sure you can actually handle them well before pushing for the salary increase).

☑ 4. **Because you're unhappy with your job.**

Making more money isn't going to make you like your job more. Instead of investing your energy in getting a higher salary for a job that you're not happy with, use that energy to find a higher-paying job in the same field, or even a job for the same amount of money that you will like. Alternately, consider looking within the company for other jobs that might be more fulfilling for you.

☑ 5. **If you've been on the job for less than six months.**

If you haven't taken on additional responsibilities or, alternately, lived up to every expectation outlined in your job description, now isn't the time. Often, employees exit college and enter the workplace with an inappropriate sense of entitlement and timing (they think a month on the job is long enough to prove their worth). This is a myth and one that can kill any chance you might have of a salary increase.

☑ **6. If you're not prepared.**
If you can't list the reasons why you deserve a raise, you're not ready to ask for one.

☑ **7. You're having a bad day.**
Don't schedule your own performance review or a meeting to ask your boss for more money if you're not feeling strong enough to handle rejection. Preparing yourself mentally is just as important as being prepared with facts and figures. If your meeting ends with you in tears, you're going to do more harm than good to your career aspirations.

☑ **8. Your boss is having a bad day.**
You should be as tuned in to your boss's ups and downs as you are your own. If she's spent the past two weeks negotiating with her boss (or taking on new projects, or handling a personal emotional crisis), she's not going to be as receptive to your request for a raise as she would be if you catch her on a good day. Sometimes the key to successful negotiation is being able to wait it out until the smoke has cleared.

☑ **9. If it isn't based on performance.**
Don't ask for a raise based on your own financial needs, such as a sudden increase in rent, the need to pay for your wedding, a bill-skipping former roommate, college loan officers beating down your door,

or any other personal reasons. Your boss doesn't want to hear your tale of financial woe. Financial hardship is tough (I still have student loans to prove it), but it's not a good reason to ask for a raise.

☑ **10. Your expectations are too high.**

Just because you ask, it doesn't mean that your boss will come through. If you have a set figure in mind and your boss isn't able to rise to the occasion, you have to be willing to meet somewhere in the middle. You have to have some flexibility in order to make headway. If asking for a 10 percent raise gets you a 5 percent increase instead, but you resent it and slack off on your job as a result, you're going to hurt your future career options.

YOU *CAN* ALWAYS GET WHAT YOU WANT
... IF YOU REALLY DESERVE IT

Okay, so you know when you should hold your tongue on asking for that raise you've desperately been salivating over for quite some time. Now it's time to figure out when the perfect opportunity to speak up is. If you're doing all your old work, plus Cube Mate Cathy's work, plus new responsibilities X, Y, and Z that your manager gave you a few months ago, you definitely deserve to be compensated for your contributions to the company. Start looking down the checklist to see if your paycheck should be going up!

☑ 1. **Summertime ... and the living is easy.**
Many companies have a fiscal year calendar that ends June 30, which means the new budget begins on July 1. If that's the case with your employer, the latter half of the year is a good time to ask.

☑ 2. **Signs of life in the job market.**
For the most part, business news bores me to tears. But if you think about it like homework in exchange for better pay, CNN Money News is easier to take. If the national job market figures report a shrinking pool of workers, your talents are going to be that much more valuable to your company because you'll be harder to replace. Do not, however, bring this up during salary negotiations. No employer wants to hear, "pay me more or I'll walk and you won't be able to replace me." And the likely response you'll get is, "walk on—we'll take our chances."

☑ 3. **You have documented proof of your fabulousness.**
You've been bringing your A game day in, day out for months. You have a great track record, additional responsibility, numerous pats on the back, and a growing collection of "way to go" e-mails from your boss. So why haven't they dropped the golden egg in your lap? Because they're waiting for you to ask. Get moving.

☑ 4. **You're confident in your abilities.**
Every boss likes an employee who is always up for a challenge, who knows she's good at what she does, and who doesn't hesitate to showcase her own achievements. Bosses sense confidence and respond to it. They want to make you happy; all you have to do is ask.

☑ 5. **You're the go-to gal.**
Don't fool yourself into thinking that you're indispensable—no one is. But if you've positioned yourself as the go-to person within your company, chances are your boss would rather pay a little more to keep you around than have to go looking for a new you.

☑ 6. **You just had a strong performance review.**
If your boss just spent an hour going over your accomplishments and singing your praises, but doesn't broach the subject of a raise, don't hesitate. Now's the time to ask. Make it simple—a "what can I expect for a pay increase this year?" is sufficient. All you have to do is open that door.

☑ **7. You have a good reason.**

Like everything else in the business world, the money you get paid is all about the value you add to the company. If your last raise was average, but you've spent the last year doing better-than-average work, your boss should be receptive to your request for a better-than-average increase.

☑ **8. Your boss just got a raise.**

You might not know for sure, but if your boss just had her performance review and is singing show tunes under her breath in the kitchen while she waits for the coffee to brew, consider it good timing for asking for a raise of your own. After all, she's the one who trained you, right?

☑ **9. Earnings are up.**

Another reason why it's important to know your industry and, specifically, how your company is doing financially. If the subject line of company-wide e-mails has changed from "we're cutting back" to "we're in the money," don't wait for another downturn before you start planning your salary review.

☑ **10. Your work load has changed.**

For the past six months, you've been taking on more and more responsibility. Maybe you're even managing staff members. Your boss doesn't hesitate to delegate, but has stealthily avoided discussing compensation. Her job is to stick to the budget (and bring it in as far under target as possible). Why should she offer you more money just because you're working harder? She shouldn't, unless you ask for it.

$\mathcal{R}esources$

GREAT READS

✳ Who cares about the money if the job is killing you? The stories in *Career Bliss: Secrets from 100 Women Who Love Their Work* by Joanne Gordon will inspire you to take the leap to a job that you love; the advice will tell you how to get there. (Ballantine Books, 2005)

✳ *Elizabeth I, CEO: Strategic Lessons from the Leader Who Built an Empire* by Alan Axelrod is a business primer based on the principles of the sixteenth-century monarch (who, besides being one of history's greatest rulers, was a single woman). (Prentice Hall, 2002)

✳ *Tough Choices: A Memoir* by former HP CEO Carly Fiorina is an inspirational story about a woman who was a liberal arts major and law school dropout who ended up running one of the country's top technology firms for six years. (Portfolio, 2006)

GREAT WEB SITES

✳ **www.ChangingCourse.com**
Thinking about a career change? Sign up for Changing Course's free biweekly e-newsletter.

✳ **www.dotcomdivas.net**
Resources for women Internet entrepreneurs.

✳ www.empowerment4women.org

Inspiration, ambition, attitude, spirit—we could all use a little Empowerment for Women.

✳ www.executivelibrary.com

Look like the office expert with these vast resources.

✳ www.fabjobs.com

Do you dream of being a stand-up comedienne? Food writer? Makeup artist? Pop star? FabJobs has how-to e-books on just about every nontraditional job you can imagine.

✳ www.globalfundforwomen.org

Working to improve women's economic independence around the world.

✳ www.goodexperience.com

Meaningful experiences in business and life. And job listings (not that you need them).

✳ www.ladieswholaunch.com

You gave the corporate world a go and decided that starting your own business is a better road to follow.

✳ www.lifehack.org

We really do want to be more productive, we just don't want a corporate consultant timing our bathroom breaks. Life-Hack is all about being better, faster, smarter—and taking the least complicated route to get there.

✳ www.marketingprofs.com

Get advice from professors and professionals on the business of marketing.

✳ www.now.org/issues/wfw/

NOW's women-friendly workplace campaign.

✳ **www.pay-equity.org**
Get salary surveys, fact sheets, and current legislation on
the wage gap from the National Committee on Pay Equity's
Web site.

✳ **www.seejanework.com**
Office supply shopping couldn't be cooler. See Jane Work or-
ganizes every successful woman.

✳ **www.springwise.com**
Get the latest trends and new business ideas sent weekly to
your e-mail inbox with Springwise newsletter: *New Business
Ideas for Entrepreneurial Minds.*

✳ **www.switchboard.com**
Yellow pages, reverse phone lookup, zip codes, and more.

✳ **www.teleworker.org**
Working from home (or want to)? Get tips, tricks and trends.

✳ **www.wageproject.org**
At its current rate of change, the wage gap won't be elimi-
nated until 2039. Unless you can afford to wait, it's time to
take a stand. Visit this Web site to find out how.

✳ **www.wiseupwomen.org**
Wi$e Up! Everything you need to know about planning for
your future.

✳ **www.womenwork.org**
Advances women's economic self-sufficiency.

✳ **www.work4women.org**
Nontraditional occupations and the women who love them.

ADDITIONAL RESOURCES MENTIONED:

* Catalyst, a research and advisory organization,
  www.catalyst.org.

* The Institute for Women's Policy and Research,
  www.iwpr.org.

* 9 to 5: The National Association of Working Women,
  www.9to5.org.

* Salary finders and more,
  www.salary.com.

* The U.S. Equal Employment Opportunity Commission,
  www.eeoc.gov.

Acknowledgments

Because women, work, and the wage gap are all topics near and dear to my heart, it's been both a pleasure and privilege to write this book. I'd like to thank-in-advance all of the working women who, one by one, will help us collectively close the wage gap. I'd also like to thank my boss, Nikki Hardin, for inspiring me to put my "rules" down on paper (among other things); my friend, coworker, and former intern, Aleigh Acerni, for informing me during her first few weeks of work that it was my job she was after; my constant reader and cheerleader, Katie Foote; all of the spectacular women I work with every day at *skirt!* magazine—they inspire me endlessly; my oldest and dearest friend Mary Kathryn Green for inspiring several of the anecdotes in this book (and for listening to my B.S. for the past fourteen-odd years); Michael Culler for his friendship and emotional support through three job transitions (to date); Jennet Robinson Alterman at The Center for Women in Charleston; Alison Piepmeier, director of Women's and Gender Studies at the College of Charleston; Mary Norris and Kaleena Cote at skirt! books for their honing, editing, and encouragement; and of course, my mother, my sisters, my nieces, and all of the other amazing women in my life. you ROCK my world.